BEYOND
TEARS

Front cover: A group of Zimbabwe 'war veterans' prepare their evening meal in their newly erected squatter camp on the occupied farm Greenspan in the Chinoyi district. *(AP Photo/Rob Cooper)*

This book is for my son Richard and all the children of Zimbabwe. It is for you that we speak out.

First they came for the Jews and I did not speak out
because I was not a Jew.
Then they came for the communists and I did not speak out
because I was not a communist.
Then they came for the trade unionists and I did not speak out
because I was not a trade unionist.
Then they came for me –
and there was no one left to speak out for me.

Pastor Niemoller (Nazi victim)

BEYOND TEARS

ZIMBABWE'S TRAGEDY

CATHERINE BUCKLE

JONATHAN BALL PUBLISHERS
JOHANNESBURG & CAPE TOWN

Published by
JONATHAN BALL PUBLISHERS (PTY) LTD
P O Box 33977
Jeppestown
2043

ISBN 1 86842 139 2

Design by Michael Barnett, Johannesburg
Typesetting and reproduction of cover by TripleM Design & Advertising, Johannesburg
Typesetting and reproduction of text by HRH Graphics, Centurion
Printed and bound by CTP Book Printers, Caxton Street, Parow, Cape

CONTENTS

FOREWORD

C athy Buckle could easily have written this book from exile. After she had been driven off her Stow Farm near Marondera, she could have packed her belongings and her family and headed for either South Africa, Canada, the United Kingdom, Australia or New Zealand. These are solidly democratic Commonwealth countries who would have given her sanctuary.

She did not flee from the country of her birth. Her first book was a bold attempt to narrate the terrifying events that occurred in Zimbabwe after the 2000 constitutional referendum, the first in independent Zimbabwe. What followed the result of that referendum has been chronicled elsewhere. But Cathy Buckle's latest book has the immediacy of an eyewitness account. She does write with passion and emotion. It would take superhuman control of one's emotions to be able to write of the events since 2000 without a display of passion. People have been killed, most of them unarmed and innocent, men, women and children. Women have been raped, some by people young enough to be their children. Men have been bludgeoned to death for no other reason than that they have dared to raise their voices against a tyranny that nobody had foreseen at independence in 1980.

The promises of a land flowing with milk and honey have almost been dashed. A regime so wrapped up in its own importance has unleashed a reign of terror which has left few sectors unscathed – farmers, journalists, the clergy, trade unionists, lawyers, judges, politicians, bankers, business people, human rights activists, gays and lesbians, novelists, actors and playwrights. Add to that list ordinary people going about the business of trying to survive a political and economic system steeped in terror and you have a country teetering on the brink of civil war or total economic collapse.

It is important to remember that had the people not rejected the draft constitution proposed by President Mugabe's Zanu PF government in the referendum of February 2000 the bloodshed of the last two years would not have occurred.

Zanu PF had ruled the country for 20 years without so much as a whimper of protest from most of the people. Attempts had been made by courageous men and women of principle to remove the Zanu PF government from power through the ballot box. Joshua Mqabuko Nkomo had tried, but had failed. In the end, declaring he would not become another Jonas Savimbi, the Angolan rebel who led his Unita movement in a 27-year guerrilla war against the MPLA government, Nkomo left Zimbabwe. After a brief stay in exile in the early 1980s, Nkomo returned to the country for which he had sacrificed the comforts of life, to sign a unity accord with Mugabe in 1987, ending a bloody civil war which had raged in Matabeleland and Midlands.

Mugabe consolidated his power by a constitutional amendment that made him an executive rather than a ceremonial president. The rest is history: as Edgar Tekere once protested, before he was kicked out of Zanu PF, 'democracy is in the intensive care unit'. In 1990, Tekere himself stood against Mugabe in the presidential election and lost. His performance was by no means lacklustre. In many ways, he showed that the beast that was Zanu PF could be destroyed in its lair.

Zanu PF had become a political beast, lashing out at voices of dissent, including the unions, the media and the clergy. By 2000, enough dissent had built up for the government to be forced to stage a constitutional referendum during which the people were to decide how they wanted to be governed in the future – whether under the straitjacket Marxism-Leninism of Zanu PF or under another political system which could ensure their freedom from being butchered or imprisoned if they so much as whispered dissent against Zanu PF.

The people said No to Zanu PF, but particularly to Mugabe's continued presidency. Like me, Cathy Buckle must remember the moment of Mugabe's moment of utter humiliation with some relish. The giant had been reduced to a dwarf. All the quiet braggadocio which he displayed every time he appeared on TV had been dissipated by the rejection of his draft constitution by the people. There had been a revolution against his revolution, which had brought independence to Zimbabwe in 1980. The people had said No to his proposal to tie them hand and foot to his regime with its demand for total and unquestioning loyalty to, basically, the one-party system of government.

Cathy Buckle has catalogued with relative dispassion the brutality with which the so-called war veterans went about terrorising the commercial farmers and their workers. But in the whole country itself ordinary people felt the wrath of the rejection. By the time the June 2000 parliamentary elections came around, the country was totally polarised. As a journalist at the only independent newspaper in the country, the fledgling *Daily News*, I too felt the heat, along with such gallant journalists as Geoff Nyarota, the editor, and his deputy, Davison Maruziva. Our reporters and photographers bore the brunt of the wrath of the so-called war veterans. They were a ragtag group ostensibly faithful to the principles that had driven them to the struggle. But in reality it appeared that all they were after were the spoils from the seizure of the farms. They killed and raped with an impunity matched only by the government's utter refusal to rein them in.

But in the middle of all this mayhem, people of courage emerged and it is to these people that Zimbabwe might eventually owe its survival from the brutality of Mugabe's regime. The same people he has persecuted, including the likes of Cathy Buckle and other whites who have remained in the country and decided its future is worth fighting for, may turn the tide against the state terror unleashed on the country.

International action in solidarity with the people has been essential. There are many who believe that the United States, the European Union, the Commonwealth and indeed the United Nations itself should have acted more decisively against the Mugabe regime. Smart sanctions have not really hurt the regime. Mugabe would be justified in borrowing a phrase used years ago by a British Member of Parliament to describe an attack by a political opponent as 'like being savaged by a butterfly'.

The people of Zimbabwe, reeling under the ravages of an economy run by a political party willing to squander every state cent on its own survival in power, are willing to make the ultimate sacrifice. They have endured so much pain and suffering under this regime that real tough and unrelenting sanctions would not cow them, if they would eventually lead to the destruction of the regime, or its capitulation. As they have said in Shona many times *Kusiri kufa ndekupi?* (Would any other death be different from this?)

One misconception among some people around the world is that the conflict in Zimbabwe is utterly racial in nature. This is not necessarily true. What is true is that Mugabe and his party tried in vain to whip up racial emotions to win their battle. The last chapter of Cathy Buckle's book narrates her disappointment with people she had not expected to rejoice at the illegal seizure of farms from white commercial farmers. For me, this made very depressing reading. But this is the truth. Mugabe has managed to convince some black Zimbabweans that as long as his action consists of depriving whites of property and giving it to the blacks, it can be justified on the grounds that this is an essential rectification of a colonial wrong – white took from black and now black must take from white what he took from him.

Some quite intelligent blacks have been taken in by this ruse. Others, more perceptive, and the majority, have managed to see beyond this simplistic and bogus theory. What they know is the character of the regime, that it is so determined to remain in power, it will do absolutely anything to achieve this goal, if it means killing, raping and maiming as many people as are willing to throw themselves in its path towards its goal.

Such people know that, like all dictatorships in the past, this regime will fight to the last breath before it gives up power. What it needs to force it to capitulate is the people's absolute resistance to its every attempt to cow them. In their favour must be the history of the liberation struggle itself. Contrary to the attempts by Zanu PF to portray itself as having won the war entirely by itself, the people know that without their active support, in the cities and towns and in the villages, the freedom fighters would never have achieved the successes which later convinced the Smith regime that only dialogue would end the war. But it is true, as Cathy Buckle's last chapter shows poignantly, that there are people, black and white, quite willing to blithely ignore the lessons of history and sup with the devil in the forlorn hope that they too can benefit from the spoils.

People like Cathy Buckle, white, young and well educated, could easily have decided to go with the flow, to let sleeping dogs lie, to do what they could to extract from the situation what they could and hope to continue their lives with the same luxury to which they were accustomed – and to hell with the rest of the people. Fortunately for Zimbabwe, there are many like Cathy Buckle.

At the time of writing, the government had spoken of the final chapter in its land reform programme. By August 2002, there will be very few white people farming in this country. In July, most of them were expected to have ceased farming and to be confined to their homesteads on the farms. By August, they will be expected to have left the farms, leaving them to the settlers – and heaven knows what fate for the future of agriculture in the country.

But the more immediate question must revolve around the political future of the country. The international community needs to maximise its sanctions against the regime. Travel restrictions are a cosmetic and utterly ineffective way of punishing Mugabe for claiming to have won a free and fair presidential election. It is time for the United Nations Security Council to be brought into the picture. There are provisions which can be used to suspend Zimbabwe's membership from the UN, and thus prevent him from using the UN to travel around the world as if he did not carry this political and highly contagious virus of despotism and brutality against his own people.

As a journalist working in Zimbabwe under a law which makes my profession a crime, I might be accused of being unfairly biased against the Mugabe regime. But I am forced to recall how journalism was during my early career, in the late 1950s. Yes, the regime then was racist, but the *African Daily News*, on which I cut my journalistic teeth beginning in 1957, enjoyed much more freedom than the *Daily News* does today in Zimbabwe.

It may sound like a horrible thing to say today, but most people in this country are not excited about their political independence as long as Zanu PF is in power. This party has made independence a symbol of black-on-black repression which has persuaded many blacks to believe that not all black leaders who led their countries to independence should be allowed to continue their leadership after independence. Was it not Nelson Mandela who said former liberation war leaders make the worst post-independence leaders in Africa? And would anyone in Zimbabwe today disagree with the observation by Desmond Tutu that Mugabe is a caricature of the African leader?

For the record, at the time of writing I had never met Cathy Buckle in person, but since we started publishing her column regularly I have come to respect her, not only as a woman who has endured and survived torture of the worst kind, but also as a commentator with compassion and the sharp wit to make the reading of her column enjoyable, even if the subject is one sad enough to bring tears to your eyes. I am confident that this, her second book on the terrible state of our country, will inspire all of us in Zimbabwe to believe that the future is not entirely lost yet. The milk and honey is bound to start flowing again soon.

Bill Saidi
Assistant Editor and columnist
Daily News, Harare

INTRODUCTION

In 1990, my husband and I bought Stow Farm in Marondera, Zimbabwe. The property, 1 000 acres (433 hectares) in extent, is located on poor, rocky soil and not suitable for cropping. As was the law in Zimbabwe in 1990, when a farm came on the market it was first offered to the government either for redistribution to peasants or for resettlement purposes. In March 1990 we received a Certificate of No Interest: the Zimbabwean government said in writing that it did not want Stow Farm and that we were free to purchase the property and commence agricultural operations.

The farm was extremely run down and we knew that we had a long road ahead of us to get it up and running. We borrowed money from a finance house, agreeing to monthly and annual repayments with an 18 per cent interest rate. Within a year the interest rate had soared to 46 per cent and servicing the debt became an enormous and often unbearable burden. As the payment date arrived each month we were forced to sell more and more of our personal belongings in order to keep the farm. Ian had no choice but to find work outside Zimbabwe and I ran the farm alone, continually living on the breadline in a collapsing and very dilapidated house.

It took us seven years to pay off the loan, but by 1997 Stow Farm was completely ours and we were free of debt. For the next three years we continued to sink every cent we had into the farm. By now our only son had been born and we were determined that Stow Farm would be his legacy for the future. Ian continued to work away from the farm and his income paid the bills and secured a respectable herd of breeding cattle. At home alone, I built up a flock of breeding sheep, established a number of timber plantations, built chicken runs and reared broilers and layers. I bought a few dairy cows and sold milk and home-made butter in our small but thriving trading store. I started a greenhouse and grew both house plants and herbs for sale in Marondera town and developed a sizeable market for the produce grown in our fruit and vegetable garden.

It had been an extremely tough and uphill battle, but by 2000 Ian and I were at last beginning to reap the benefits. Stow Farm had become a viable and productive property; we had begun renovating the house, removing the white ants from the ceilings and replacing the leaking roof. We had electrified the workers' housing, plumbed in piped water to the staff complex and were finally beginning to find our feet. A decade of work and huge personal sacrifice ended on 28 February 2000, when a mob of men arrived at our farm gate and claimed that the property and everything on it belonged to them. They said they were veterans of the 1980 War for Independence and had come to take back what had been stolen from their ancestors.

Stow Farm, like hundreds of other Zimbabwean farms, had been invaded, and there was absolutely nothing we could do about it. President Mugabe, desperate for his Zanu PF (Zimbabwe African National Union – Patriotic Front) party to remain in power, had played the last two cards in his hand: land and race, and he would not instruct the police to remove the land invaders. He was adamant that the land belonged to the people and said that the invasions were nothing more than peaceful demonstrations by land-hungry peasants and war veterans. Even with video footage of the war veterans receiving payments from government officials for their occupation of Stow Farm, which had not been gazetted for government seizure, we had no one to turn to for help. The police became increasingly partisan, war veterans were promoted to senior ranks in the security forces and the country was in the grip of anarchy.

We had become pawns in the middle of an evil political game. Stow Farm became a war veterans' base camp and headquarters and for the following seven months Ian, Richard and I – and all the men, women and children who lived and worked on Stow Farm – endured the terror, intimidation and violence. We were not alone in our hell: on hundreds of other farms thousands of workers were beaten and harassed, farmers were murdered and anyone suspected of supporting the opposition MDC (Movement for Democratic Change) became a target for violence and a victim of Zanu PF.

The story of my family's hell and the unfolding crisis in Zimbabwe in the year 2000 is told in *African Tears*. *Beyond Tears* is a sequel to that book and an eye-witness account of Zimbabwe's descent into total economic collapse and famine. It begins in January 2001 and outlines the systematic destruction of Zimbabwe by a government determined to retain power, revealing some of the horrors other farmers have endured and their desperate struggle to keep growing food for the country.

Cathy Buckle
July 2002

ONE

OUT OF THE ASHES

When I left Stow Farm in September 2000 I had no idea what I was going to do, where I would go or how I would earn my living. I thought my involvement with farms, war veterans and the evil politics of Zimbabwe had come to an end, but as the months passed I discovered how wrong I was. I had no idea that I would get even more involved with the horrors on farms – that I would find myself becoming a spokesperson for hundreds of people whose stories of savagery and barbaric behaviour needed to be told.

Being physically removed from the daily hell of harassment and threats on my own doorstep gave me a chance to breathe and look at the broader crisis in Zimbabwe. When I put things into perspective and saw the depth and enormity of it all I was shocked almost beyond words – but I knew that these stories had to be told. There was not a home in Zimbabwe, rural or urban, rich or poor, black or white, that had not been affected by the politics of the country. There were very few people who did not have a relation, friend or colleague who had suffered abuse at the hands of people who called themselves war veterans, whose numbers later grew to include government supporters, Zanu PF youth brigade, Border Gezi graduates or simply 'militants'.

The Border Gezi graduates, also known as 'Green Bombers', are youths who were trained under the Ministry of Youth at camps around the country. They are called the Gezi boys because this was the brainchild of the late Minister of Youth, Border Gezi. According to the government, they were re-educated, given a sense of national pride and responsibility, and taught about Zimbabwe's past and the history of liberation and the role of Zanu in this. They were given three months' training, issued with green overalls and sent out around the country to campaign for Zanu PF.

The Gezi boys were the ones who set up roadblocks, demanded Zanu PF party cards and beat up and tortured hundreds of people. They are largely implicated in a great deal of the violence. The Gezi boys were all promised that if Zanu PF won the elections they would be given jobs in the police and army, but reports coming in subsequently indicate they feel they have been deserted; the jobs have not materialised and they are increasingly angry as they discover they were used. The government has recently stated that any youth now wanting to apply for a position in our civil service has to undergo the three months' training at the Border Gezi camp.

It was terrifying to live in a country that was making history in the bloodiest of ways, but every single day there were encounters with the most incredible people. Perhaps the most remarkable thing about living in a country without law and order was the revelation of the totally unexpected goodness of ordinary people. It was the most enlightening experience to see another side of people, to let the labels fall away and the preconceived ideas and beliefs dissolve, to suddenly discover that they are not actually important and that things and people are seldom as they seem.

Leaving the farm was a watershed for me. It forced me to re-evaluate every aspect of my life and my place in Zimbabwe. I had no idea how deeply affected my seven-year-old son had been by months of living on an invaded farm or how deep the psychological scars were. I would discover that it would take a lot of work and love to erase them and make him feel safe and secure again. There were so many adjustments we were both going to have to make, and an awful lot of heartache to face, endure and survive.

Leaving our farm and family home was a drop in the ocean of losses Richard and I would have to try and come to terms with. Richard lost not only the only home he had ever known, but also his freedom, independence and friends. For the first seven years of his life he had spent all his waking hours outside. When he stepped out of the front door he was amongst geese that hissed and chased him, orphan lambs that followed him around and sucked on his fingers, calves that ran around him in giddy circles with tails curled over their backs. His playground had always been in home-made forts in the bush, his toys were bows and arrows made out of twigs and bark and his exercise was swinging on saplings and climbing fence poles. Encounters with his friends were often spent sitting in the dust outside one of the workers' houses, eating sadza with his fingers and dipping thick chunks of bread into tin mugs of sweet tea. They made cars out of pram wheels and old tins and pushed one another around in wheelbarrows.

All of their adventures had been around the farm, riding in the ox-cart sitting atop hay or firewood. Whenever I went out of the door on the farm Richard and his friends piled into the back of my truck, knowing we were heading for thrills and excitement. Wherever I went the children followed, guaranteed both drama and fun, whether I was delivering stock feed, carrying poles, cutting off lambs' tails and testicles or doing a job down at the dam. Richard and his friends caught crabs in the mud with home-made fishing rods and ran screaming and laughing at any rustle in the grass as a snake or leguaan, hare or mongoose emerged. There was always laughter, which was mostly at my expense as a cow knocked me down, a ram butted me or a lamb peed on me. Their amusement would turn into hysteria if I slipped in a cowpat or had to run and climb over a fence if one of the bulls was having a bad day. All of these things were as safe and familiar for Richard as they were for me, but now everything would have to change. Everyone told me that Richard was young, that children are tough survivors and he would soon adapt, but this enormous turmoil was just the beginning for him and indeed for us as a family.

Very soon after we left the farm the psychological effects of seven months of harassment and hell at the hands of war veterans took their toll on us all. I was forty-two, but felt and looked decades older. My face was blotched with skin cancer from years in the sun; my hands were creased, cracked and thick with calluses. For months I had incessant thrush and lived on one prescription after another. I began putting off washing my hair as great handfuls fell out. The dentist's surgery became almost my second home as one after another my teeth cracked and chipped. I finally began to believe my doctor's words about the effects of prolonged stress.

My 18-year marriage to Ian collapsed and within a few months of leaving the farm we were divorced, both tossed in the anguish of what had happened to us, our home, our lives and plans. We both began the long and torturous task of starting both our homes and lives again – an almost overwhelming burden. I buried myself in work and put everything I had into my son and my writing. I hoped my book *African Tears* could be the start of a new life and career and give Richard and me the security we both so desperately needed. For a decade I had been a full-time farmer and part-time writer. I had never had a non-fiction work published before – but with four novels under my belt, I was determined to give my best. Gradually every surface of the house was covered in mountains of paper as I tackled the enormous job of fact-gathering and research.

I limped my way into the New Year, still struggling to adapt to living in a town. The smallest of things gave me sleepless nights. Almost the first thing I did on moving into a rented house in my home town was to install an electric fence on top of the wall which surrounded the half-acre property. I knew that this was not my property and that it was not an expense I would be able to recover, but it was worth it just for peace of mind. I'd received many electric shocks on the fence that had surrounded our farmhouse and knew that it was an enormous deterrent. These four thin wires also gave Richard a feeling of safety and would hopefully be the first step in helping him recover from the huge traumas of the previous year.

The first day the fence was up and working Richard sat on the steps with me in the evening as we had tea together.

'I'm glad we've got the electric fence, Mum,' he said.

'Are you, Rich?'

'Yes, cos I know no one can get in now,' he said.

He rubbed his little hands together and looked up at me. 'Don't you remember how sore it is, Mum? That time I forgot and touched it on the farm and it knocked me down?'

Putting my arm round Richard's shoulder, I hugged him. I did remember that day very well: how he had come inside, white as a sheet, shaking and crying, and how awful I'd felt.

'No one's going to get in here, Rich,' I said. 'We haven't got a night guard any more, but we have got the electric fence and the dogs and we are going to be really safe here.'

Richard didn't comment and I prayed that this time his trust in my words would not be misplaced. After all, I had told him on the farm that the police would come and help us with the war veterans, and they hadn't. I had told him that after the elections the war veterans squatting all over our farm would go away, and they hadn't. I had told him that no one would ever hurt me or the people who worked for us, and someone had. I had told him that we would never leave our farm, and we had. So many lies I had told my son. I didn't know how I would ever repair the damage – but perhaps this was the starting point.

I hoped that the electric fence would help drive away my sleepless nights and Richard's nightmares, but knew it wouldn't help me to get used to sleeping in what seemed like bright daylight. Outside the house was a street lamp and the light from it was so bright after the absolute darkness of the farm, that most nights I would toss and turn for hours and long for a power cut. One morning the bank's PR lady, after commenting on my obvious exhaustion and the huge rings under my eyes, gave me the solution to the problem. I hung the thickest, heaviest, darkest blanket I could find in the window, hooking it into the burglar bars. The heat was abominable but the darkness was pure bliss.

The night noises in town were so different too. I had been used to hearing owls and the contracting of the tin roof on the farm; now I had to get used to car hooters, dogs barking and the distant roar of the night train leaving the station. What gave me the most sleepless nights, though, was my mind, which went round and round with a million things crowding into my consciousness, demanding my attention and rational explanations.

All around there was madness and mayhem. Every election, whether for government, council or mayoral positions, was accompanied by a terrible degree of violence as war veterans and government supporters overran huge areas and did whatever they thought necessary to terrify the opposition into voting for Zanu PF or not voting at all.

When the Bikita by-election in January was won by Zanu PF, the usual gloating and victory rallies faded into insignificance as news came in that the president of the Democratic Republic of the Congo had been assassinated. There was uproar, and government propaganda went crazy. Initial reports came in through the BBC, then from Reuters. Laurent Kabila had apparently been shot by one of his bodyguards.

The world said that Kabila was dead; Zimbabwe said he was not. Minister of Defence Moven Mahachi said that Laurent Kabila had been flown from the Congo to Harare for emergency medical treatment but had been dead on arrival in Harare. Minister of Information Jonathan Moyo, however, said that he was not dead. There was complete and utter chaos and confusion and it soon became clear that neither the Congo nor Zimbabwe was ready to officially announce the death of the president. An aircraft from the Congo was seen at Harare Airport, speculation intensified and rumours were rife. It seemed that while our Defence Minister had officially announced the death of Kabila, the Congolese authorities had not. Zimbabweans were close to hysteria with the conflicting reports and complete mess our government was making of it all.

The *Zimbabwe Independent* helped shed light on the matter. 'High level military sources said the fiasco – probably one of the greatest public relations disasters surrounding the death of a president in recent history – followed President Mugabe's secret arrangement with the Congolese military high command ... Mugabe was anxious to delay confirming Kabila's death ... to put in place firm security arrangements before announcing the president's death. So Kabila was kept officially "alive" and Harare agreed to maintain the deceit. Officials apparently forgot to tell Mahachi.' So, with two top Zimbabwean ministers contradicting each other, there was nothing to do except wait.

I could not help but smile at the way the *Zimbabwe Independent* described Jonathan Moyo's behaviour. The journalist said that he had 'retreated into obfuscation' in line with the government's plans to fudge the news. I was reminded of Monty Python's classic comedy, in which a customer and a pet shop owner argue about a parrot that is nailed to its wooden perch and is clearly dead. The more the pet shop owner tries to assure the customer that the parrot is not dead but just resting, the angrier John Cleese gets. Finally he explodes: 'This is an ex-parrot. He's turned up his tootsies, gone to meet his maker. He's f...ing snuffed it.' Laurent Kabila was dead: both the Congolese and Zimbabwean governments knew it, and had finally to admit his mortality. Zimbabweans wondered what this would do to 11 000 of our soldiers in the Congo. Would the war now end or escalate, would our soldiers finally come home, would the endless drain on our economy finally come to an end? No one knew – and as always, President Mugabe said not one word.

The death affected my little home town of Marondera in an unbelievable and frightening way. A group of men were having a long and predominantly liquid lunch in the golf pub at the Marondera Country Club. One man apparently raised his glass and proposed a toast to the demise of Laurent Kabila. This sentiment was not unique to Marondera, but such expressions were not acceptable. Moments after the toast had been raised, the club was overrun by war veterans. Senior school students having golf instruction on the green had to run and scramble under a fence to get away from the marauders. Laurent Kabila had been President Mugabe's greatest friend and ally and an insult to the Congolese leader was an insult to his Zimbabwean counterpart, they said. The man who had raised his glass was promptly arrested, all the patrons of the club were ordered to leave and war veterans took over the small establishment.

Armed war veterans then barricaded the road into the Marondera Club with drums, planted a Zimbabwe flag in the driveway and would not let anyone in. A hand-painted sign appeared on the roadside: 'The Laurent Kabila Memorial Club'. Police and passers-by left the veterans alone and they proceeded to clean out the contents of the kitchen and bar – and then, a week later, disappeared back into the woodwork. It was not safe anywhere now.

My courage in speaking out (if that is what it was) was seriously shaken when the printing presses of the *Daily News* were bombed on 28 January 2001. In the early hours of the morning a cream Mazda truck was seen at the printing factory in the Lochinvar industrial sites in Harare. The numberplates were noted by security guards who ran for their lives as the printing presses were blown to smithereens. In the following days officials refused to release information concerning the ownership of the truck, saying it was sensitive, and no arrests were made at all. Five days later journalists held a protest march in Harare condemning the bombing, but they were swiftly dealt with by riot police who immediately broke up the demonstration. All the circumstances surrounding the bombing and supposed investigations were suspicious in the extreme.

This was the first step in a renewed onslaught to silence the voices of dissent that were getting louder in Zimbabwe. I was one of those voices and many people begged me to stop speaking out, but I could not. I wasn't writing or fighting to preserve a way of life but to speak out for the thousands of people who were too scared to do so for themselves. I wanted people to know and understand what was going on in Zimbabwe. More than anything, I wanted to stay in what I had always thought of as my country – and if speaking out might help end this nightmare, then that was what I would do. Some days, the task of getting the information out was exhausting, especially when something in the Marondera water supply made me and most of the town extremely ill.

It had taken me a couple of months to get used to drinking water that did not come straight from the ground to my tap. Our water on the farm had not been treated at all; it just came straight from the borehole to the house – no chlorine or fluoride, just raw, pure water. In town it came from big storage reservoirs that were supplied by the town dam. For well over a month, hundreds of people had fallen ill with what became known as 'Marondera diarrhoea'. It was awful, totally debilitating – the type that necessitated moving your bed into the toilet. None of the usual over-the-counter drugs had any effect whatsoever and every surface of my house was littered with pills and potions, concoctions and mixtures.

After a week in which I staggered from the bed to the lavatory and endured the most hideous cramps, the diarrhoea disappeared. I was one of the lucky ones, though: soon there were no drugs to buy and two people in the town died. At one point in the week I had managed to get to the doctor and was told that the inspection hatch on top of the Marondera storage reservoir had been removed. Apparently monkeys and baboons drank at this opening and a dead animal had been found in the water. This was another sign illustrating the collapse of public services in Zimbabwe.

January had been an awful month for the country, with murder, bombings and disease. War veterans remained on farms and there was more and more evidence that land invasions were being instigated by people in high places. Reports poured in of city dwellers, some of them obviously wealthy businessmen, driving luxury vehicles, arriving on commercial farms at weekends to claim bits of someone else's land. There was no one farmers could turn to and nothing they could do except watch helplessly as the nightmare went on. Fresh in everyone's minds was the murder of commercial farmer Henry Elsworth, barely a month before. Ambushed at his Kwekwe farm, the 70-year-old man was shot in the stomach as he got out to open the gate. He died a few minutes later. His son, Ian, who was driving the car, was shot nine times in the foot, thighs, hips and arm.

The fear continued and there was no end in sight. War veterans reigned supreme in rural areas and were stepping up their reign of terror in towns too. The world seemed to have stopped watching and no one commented when, four days before the end of January, the government published another list of 133 farms to be compulsorily acquired. There was no sense to it, but it seemed that our government was determined to continue on this catastrophic path it had chosen. Making sense of the politics became a full-time job: I am sure that if we ever knew the truth of what was really going on, the story would have been an immediate bestseller. Fear was increasing, though, and fewer and fewer people – whether black or white – were speaking out.

Coping with the stress and fear became almost intolerable. The situation was exacerbated for me when the *Sunday Times* newspaper in England heard of the imminent release of *African Tears* and asked for serialisation rights. I went into cold panic. Until then I had thought that perhaps my story would appeal to a few thousand Zimbabweans – but here were complete strangers to Africa showing an enormous interest. This should have been the absolute highlight of my writing career. Having your work serialised by one of the world's top newspapers should be cause for massive celebration and wild popping of champagne corks. Instead, I went into a state of almost catatonic paralysis. It suddenly dawned on me that my book was going to be read by people all over the world and that now, whether I liked it or not, I had moved into a position of high profile. Success was indeed bittersweet: that night I cried myself to sleep.

As the date for the serialisation of *African Tears* in the *Sunday Times* approached I became more and more tense. Everywhere I went, I paid particular attention to people sitting around; I watched my rear view mirror incessantly when I drove to and from school and made sure that someone knew where I was all the time. I never went anywhere without my cell phone, not even on my little Sunday afternoon outings with Richard.

Ever since we had left the farm one of the things Richard missed most was the space to ride his bicycle. 'I need a big place, Mum,' he said, 'so I can go fast and feel the wind.' Richard, like me, loved the wind, and the garden in our rented house in Marondera was just too small for him to get up any speed. Every Sunday we would walk across to the little cemetery down the road and while I sat on a big rock at the corner, Richard rode faster and faster circuits around the cemetery car park, the quiet filled with his laughter and shouts of delight. Perhaps it was irreverent, I thought, but then what nicer sound is there than that of a child's laughter and excitement?

Sundays became very special days, but also times when I was filled with regret and longing for the life that I had lost. The cemetery looks out over a very beautiful African vlei with Msasa trees in the distance and it always made me think of the farm, gave me that feeling of being part of nature. Whenever I could tear Richard away from his circuits around the car park, we would walk down into the vlei and look at the grasses and wild flowers. In February all the grasses are in full flower and covered with seed heads bursting with new life, beige and cream, green and pink. I knew almost all the Latin and common names of the grasses and Richard and I would bend down, feel their silky, fluffy or scratchy heads and repeat the strange names that were used to identify each one as different from the next. I was delighted as my son saw and commented on things that had so much meaning for me too. 'It looks like waves, Mum,' he would say as the wind swept through the vlei, making the grasses bend and flow.

Perhaps Africa was already in my son's blood too – and there was so much for him to see and learn in the years ahead. Too much for me to give in to the fear that had temporarily paralysed my typing fingers. I went back to work with renewed vigour and tried not to think about what would happen when my name hit the pages of an English newspaper. I kept hoping that more and more people would start speaking out and relieve some of the pressure, but it didn't happen. Everyone always had an excuse as to why they did and said nothing. Businessmen said that if they were critical they might lose government tenders. Civil servants said that if they made waves they would lose their jobs. Individuals said that if they spoke out it might attract the wrath of war veterans. Everyone was waiting for someone else to be 'the one.'

Being 'the one' had become the national pastime in Zimbabwe. From government ministers to police spokesmen and civil servants, the standard response to any problem or issue was: 'I am not the one.' Passing the buck at every level in our society was a mirror image of events in the country. As the economy collapsed, the government was 'not the one', so it blamed the whites. As violence flared up on farms, war veterans were 'not the ones', so they blamed the farmers. When there was no foreign currency to buy fuel, the National Oil Company of Zimbabwe was 'not the one', so it blamed whites for hoarding petrol. When political violence flared up and people were killed and tortured, Zanu PF was 'not the one', so it blamed the opposition. The whites and the opposition, it appeared, were The One, and as the months passed we were blamed for every aspect of Zimbabwe's complete collapse.

When February came to an end I was The One, and was forced to face one of the most painful horrors that had become so commonplace in Zimbabwe. Emmanuel Sunday, a loyal and dedicated employee of mine for a decade, was dying of Aids. Emmanuel, or as Richard called him, Manuel, had started working for me on the farm in 1991. He was a superb fencer but had a great weakness for alcohol. A couple of months after he had started a big fencing contract for me on the farm, he went into town one night to have a few drinks. While waiting on the side of the road for a lift back to the farm, Manuel was struck down by a hit-and-run driver and his arm was broken very badly from the wrist to the elbow. He did not receive the best of treatment at our local hospital and came away with little use of his badly disfigured arm. He was never able to wield the fencing pliers or strainers after that and for weeks after the accident sat in a relation's house getting thinner and thinner until I heard of his plight.

Manuel became my right-hand man, doing all the jobs I didn't have time for. He tended the chickens, watered the vegetable garden, trundled backwards and forwards to the store and then, when Richard was born, he became my son's best friend. Perhaps, to the outsider, this sounds like a very patronising tale, but it was and is the face and fact of Africa. Manuel had little education and had been a farm worker most of his life. After the accident he was unemployable; there just were no jobs aside from agriculture at which he could make a living. When Richard was born Manuel would help me to calm him by pushing the pram and later the pushchair. As Richard grew up he followed Manuel everywhere with a little wooden hoe and toy wheelbarrow. The two were always together and often Richard would go and have tea or lunch at Manuel's house. Manuel taught him about African music, taught him how to squat over a Blair (pit) toilet, taught him which berries were safe to eat, and taught him his first hesitant words of Shona.

When war veterans invaded our farm, Manuel's future, like that of all my other employees, hung in the balance. After a decade of being part of our family I could not abandon Manuel. He had nowhere to go and so he came with me to our rented house in Marondera, where he tended the garden, had a lovely little cottage and led a very easy life. Manuel was dying, though, and as the months passed he got weaker and weaker. He was always fighting one infection or another. He had repeated bouts of pneumonia, bronchitis and diarrhoea, and in the mornings would stagger out of bed to play with Richard for half an hour before school and then go back to bed the moment I drove out of the gate.

For weeks I battled with my conscience. I was already struggling to survive, living off rapidly dwindling savings. Rocketing inflation, not having the farm to earn a living from and still helping all the other workers from the farm was becoming an enormous financial burden. One of the men who had worked for us on Stow Farm had died of Aids and helping with the funeral expenses was the least I could do. Another had been unemployed for over a year and regularly came to my gate asking for help with food and school fees for his large family. Jane, my friend and store-keeper on the farm, had been reduced to selling bananas and tomatoes on the side of the road. She too had needed money for school fees and uniforms, for food and rent.

Whenever I went grocery shopping I bought as much as I could afford to keep Manuel strong, including fruit, vegetables, fresh milk and bread. I always paid for all the drugs, anti-diarrhoea medication, antibiotics and tonics that were needed as he fought an almost incessant stream of infections. But he lost more and more weight, got weaker and weaker, coughed blood and then became anorexic. I had no choice but to phone Manuel's family, who were all middle-income earners in Harare. Mr Sunday, his father, came out to Marondera one Sunday and we talked it all through. The word Aids was never mentioned, but we both agreed that the time had come for Manuel to go home, to go to Harare with his father, where his stepmother and step-brothers and sisters could take care of him and nurse him through his last days.

Saying goodbye to Emmanuel is not a day I want to remember. As I embraced him I could feel every rib and hear his rasping struggle for breath. I knew that I would never see him again.

'Go well, Manuel,' I said gently, hardly daring to pat his shoulder. He was so frail, so bent and suddenly so old.

'Stay well, Mrs Cathy,' he whispered as his father and I helped him into the car.

That was the last time I saw Emmanuel and although he died soon afterwards his memory, as his story had also unfolded in *African Tears*, would always be a part of me.

African Tears arrived in England with a bang. The *Sunday Times* published excerpts from the book on the front page of its News Review Supplement two Sundays in a row, early in March. By that time I had still not even seen the book, let alone proofread it for mistakes, and my anxiety reached fever pitch. The e-mails between me and my South African publishers flew fast and furiously and at last they scanned and mailed through an image of the front cover of my book. I was horrified at what I saw, as dot by dot, line by line, the screen of my computer revealed my life. We had discussed cover designs at length and I had expected something vaguely resembling my requested design. I expected to see a field with tall brown grass, a blue tent filled with war veterans, a Zimbabwean flag atop a leaning bamboo pole, and broken fences in the background. Instead, the cover was black, inlaid with a map of Zimbabwe and a sickle dripping blood.

'Oh, shit!' was the only thing I could say or think for a few hours – and as the reality of what I had done sank in, so too did terror. Words from Hilda Bernstein's book about the Rivonia Trials in apartheid South Africa became my immediate reality. 'Fear is not an icy hand, it is a burning acid that flows through every vein.' What had been my little story of a huge political evil had suddenly become front-page news.

'Cathy Buckle fears reprisals this weekend as she begins her personal account of the nightmare gripping Zimbabwe', read part of the headlines on the front page of the *Sunday Times* News Review. Alongside the words was the only photograph of me that I had agreed to anyone using. The photo, taken at my university graduation in 1979, had been blown up enormously.

African Tears took up the whole of the front and half of the second page of the newspaper. By mid-morning my phone was ringing incessantly. Calls came from South Africa, the UK and France as my extended family and friends woke up and saw my face and name on the front page of their Sunday newspapers. As one, sisters, uncles and strangers had only one thing to say to me: 'Get out of Zimbabwe now.'

I was really scared, but perhaps a stronger emotion was anger. What should have been my finest hour and the highlight of my career was engulfed yet again in fear. On the second week of the *Sunday Times* serialisation, the editor's boxed observation was painfully true: 'Cathy Buckle was always strong in the face of adversity. But President Mugabe's ethnic cleansers have reduced this brave woman to a weeping fugitive in her own land.'

Within 48 hours of the extracts from *African Tears* appearing in the *Sunday Times*, I was packing my car. Deciding on the things that I could not do without, which things to take and which to leave, was not a new experience for me – but it did not get any easier, either for me or for Richard. It was not a decision made lightly or easily, and I waited until the last minute before I told my son what was going on. I did not tell him that the endless telephone calls were from anxious friends begging me to leave and from journalists wanting interviews. I did not tell him that the various strange men coming and going, talking in hushed voices and leaving hurriedly, were security men.

Asking for some round-the-clock security had become a joke. The security companies wanted to know why I wanted protection and the moment I told them about the book they retreated rapidly, told me they were not prepared to get involved in political matters, and left. Everyone in the know told me to get out of sight. Most said I should leave the country. We discussed all the possible consequences: arrest, detention – or, most frightening of all, war veterans. By speaking out in *African Tears* I had made my bed; now I had to lie in it.

'We're going to go away for a while, Richie,' I said as I helped my son select clothes and pack his little bags.

'Why, Mum?'

I thought about my answer for a moment. I knew from all the times on the farm when I had fobbed him off that half-truths made him even more distressed, and decided to tell him the truth.

'Well, you know my book I wrote about the farm?'

'*African Tears*, you mean?'

I smiled, and knew that I should never underestimate this boy's understanding.

'Yes, *African Tears*!'

'So, what's the problem with it, Mum?'

'Well, Rich, there are going to be some people who don't like what I've said in the book and I think it might be nice if we just go away for a while so they don't come and ask me silly questions about it.'

'What about school, though, Mum? And it's my sports day this week.'

'I know it is, Rich, but I've already told them at school that we have got to go away, and they said it's OK. And anyway, Rich, we're not going far and we won't be gone too long.'

There were a few more questions about whether I was sure his teacher and sports coach knew, and when Richard seemed satisfied, we decided what he needed. Clothes and teddies, books and games, crayons and colouring books – everything was packed into two bags and shoved behind the seat of the car.

I told no one at all where I was going. This was my problem, and it was unfair for anyone else to be at risk because of my principles and decisions. Along with my small bag and briefcase went my cell phone and computer, and soon we were on the road. As I drove, the words on the front page of the *Sunday Times* shouted again and again inside my head: 'A weeping fugitive in her own land.' They were words that would haunt me for some time; later, when fear and anger were replaced by determination, the words of the newspaper became my strength.

Being in hiding was awful. I cried a lot, swore a lot and tried to come to terms with what I had done and what I was going to do. No one could tell me what to do. I had reached another turning point in my life and now had to face my conscience and decide if I was going to stand up and fight again or do what everyone was telling me to do – leave Zimbabwe.

After four days Richard had had enough. 'I just want to go home, Mum,' he cried, his little arms wrapped around my neck. 'Please, Mum, I just want to go home and see my friends. I miss the dogs and my things. Please, Mum, I just want to go home.'

By the fifth day I had made a decision. Thousands and thousands of e-mails had flooded my screen, so many that my hard drive had overloaded and crashed. Orders for the book were flooding in and thousands of people wrote to thank me for having spoken out. I had suddenly found my voice. I could not go now; I had started something which was to engulf me and the decision had been made for me.

Richard and I both sang and laughed as we re-packed our treasures into the car and headed home. I had so much work to do, nothing had stopped while I hid in a catatonic state. I was not going to be a weeping fugitive in my own country, I was not going to be a victim any more.

The more I looked at everything that was happening in Zimbabwe, the more sure I became that this insanity would not and could not last. Nothing was the same any more, and I knew that it never would be after this, but I became more and more convinced that we would emerge a stronger and more united country.

I had been off my farm for six months and my entire life had been turned upside down. I was still very unsure of what my role was, how I was going to earn a living and what the future held for me or my son. Day after day I was writing about the horrors, doing newspaper articles and interviews and publicising the situation in Zimbabwe – and then one day it suddenly hit me in the face. At the bottom of a newspaper article I'd written, the editor had added: 'Buckle is an author and human rights activist.' It was so strange to see those words and realise that this was what I had become.

More and more people wanted to talk to me, tell me what had happened to them. I met one of the five farmers who had been abducted and tortured by war veterans the year before and that story was one that had to be told because it, like no other, showed the depth of Zimbabwe's horror and political insanity. Arranging to meet all of the farmers involved, talking to the man who had seen his best friend murdered in cold blood, getting all of the details down on paper and coming to terms with the barbaric events took over two months and forced me to emerge from the ashes.

TWO

MUREHWA –
THE WEEKEND FROM HELL

Daisy ... Hyacinth ... Godfather. These three little words are the essence of a vibrant farming community in north-eastern Zimbabwe. Daisy, Hyacinth and the Godfather may all be television personalities, but I am sure their roles have never been as important as they were on 15 and 16 April 2000 in what many remember as the weekend from hell.

Over that weekend five farmers were abducted from a Zimbabwean police station by men calling themselves war veterans. They were taken away, beaten, tortured and left hanging on to life by the most fragile of threads. The five men had committed no crime; they were attempting to rescue a sixth farmer who had been abducted from his home. That sixth farmer was murdered, shot in cold blood, in broad daylight, in front of dozens of witnesses.

This is the story of that weekend from hell and is dedicated to the life, the loves and the memory of David Stevens.

'Daisy' is the name given by the Macheke farming community to the voluntary nurse on standby in the event of an emergency in the district. 'Hyacinth' is the woman who sits by the farm radio, records all communications and alerts other farmers to problems in the area. The Godfather is the man who co-ordinates all the security problems in an area which covers seventy-odd farms in the close-knit Macheke and Virginia district. The radio network in this district includes almost every property and demonstrates a community totally committed to and dependent on one another – a community of the most amazingly unselfish people, who literally put their lives on the line for one another every single day. Every farmer is rostered in four- and six-hour shifts to voluntarily man the radio, resolve problems and provide support and assistance to his neighbours. The skeleton of this radio network has been in place for years as a form of communication, but was perfected in March 2000 when squatters and war veterans invaded farms across Zimbabwe.

Daisy, Hyacinth and the Godfather were among the first to hear that a Macheke farmer had serious problems with men calling themselves 'war veterans'. They alerted the community and then sat and listened, in cold terror and absolute horror as the lives of their friends and neighbours were turned upside down, changed forever.

It all began shortly after dawn on Saturday, 15 April 2000. Hyacinth recorded the details almost verbatim. As the morning wore on the radio calls increased in frequency until they were almost incessant and involved dozens of different people, people desperate to try and help David Stevens when he first started telling the community of his problem. David's farm 'Arizona', like so many others, had been invaded by war veterans and squatters. There had been some sort of confrontation between David's farm workers and the squatters. David was in trouble; the police had been called and had arrested not the trespassers, squatters or war veterans, but a dozen of David's workers.

Hyacinth wrote down the details of David's radio message: *David says the police have taken his workers. The police are accusing David of inciting his workers to violence against the war veterans. David asked if Steve could intervene with the police on his behalf.*

Steve Krynauw, a farmer himself, was the full-time security liaison man in the community. His job was to communicate between farmers and the Macheke police.

At 1.25 pm Hyacinth recorded one of the last messages David Stevens transmitted on the farm radio: *David called. A whole lot of war veterans have arrived at his farm. David said there was a man coming to his gate right now and that he was going out to speak to him. John Osborne told Dave to report back as soon as possible. John Osborne told other farmers to be on standby.*

John Osborne, acting as the district co-ordinator, tried to make sure that everything was in place in the event of an emergency.

At 1.43 pm Hyacinth recorded that a number of farmers were standing by to go and help, ready and waiting the moment they were called. Hyacinth, Daisy, the Godfather and most Macheke and Virginia farmers sat by their radios and listened as farmers John Osborne and Steve Krynauw arrived at the road leading down to Arizona Farm. Hyacinth wrote down the first chilling details: *Apparently Dave has been handcuffed and the war vets have got him, are taking him away in his own vehicle ... Police are needed ...*

It was all happening very fast now and there were almost more communications than Hyacinth could cope with. Everyone wanted to help but had to wait until they were called. Hyacinth called the nurse on duty, Daisy for the day, to check that she was listening, was on standby. The nurse, like the rest of the district, was listening.

Hyacinth kept writing the reports down: *You must get the police into gear ... I'll try and stop them at the turn-off ... I spoke to the police, they said they left ten minutes ago and that the Member in Charge is with the vehicle ... Are you sure the Daisies are standing by? ...*

Few people knew what was really going on. It had become scary and confusing; it couldn't all be relayed on the radio. There were no guidelines for what to do in the event of an abduction.

Steve Krynauw and John Osborne were there. As they arrived at the turn-off into Arizona they were met by a vehicle coming out of the farm. There were two men in this car.

'They're armed,' John said to Steve.

The men in the car were hostile and aggressive. 'What do you want?' they demanded. 'Where are you going? What's your business here?'

Moments after the first car had departed, Steve and John saw David Stevens's beige Land Rover approaching. A strange man was driving; David was in the passenger seat and lifted his arms to show the handcuffs shackling his wrists. Almost immediately behind came another vehicle, a minibus with at least thirty 'war veterans' in it.

John and Steve followed this convoy of three vehicles. They had to find out where David Stevens was being taken; they had to do whatever they could to help this man, their friend and fellow farmer.

Hyacinth wrote down the details as Steve called them in: *They are turning right towards Murehwa ... Has anyone managed to raise the Murehwa police? ... Has anyone contacted the CFU? [Commercial Farmers Union] ... Report this as a stolen vehicle and an abduction ... We are still following ...*

A police roadblock could have stopped the convoy of vehicles anywhere between Macheke and Murehwa, a distance of approximately forty kilometres. Everyone tried to get the police onto that road; they tried by radio and by phone, but David Stevens, handcuffed and being abducted in his own vehicle, was as good as alone.

John stayed between 300 and 500 metres behind the convoy. He and Steve discussed getting closer but agreed that they should stay back, and do nothing to anger the war veterans. 'If we get any closer they may take it out on Dave,' they agreed.

An armed abduction in a stolen vehicle was going on in broad daylight. Many dozens of farmers and their wives were listening to the horror as it unfolded on the radio. Police in both Macheke and Murehwa confirmed that they knew what was going on but did absolutely nothing. They did not send reinforcements or set up a roadblock; they broke their solemn oath of office and did not protect or uphold the law; they did not try to save life and limb or even property.

Gary Luke was the Godfather on duty that day. He, like John and Steve, was prepared to do anything to try and help. Travelling alone, Gary drove out of his farm onto the Macheke/Murehwa road to try and find the police, to intercept them and try to make sure they were heading in the right direction. Gary located the Macheke police on the road. They did not have direct radio contact with Steve and John, but Gary did, and for this reason he followed the police vehicle towards Murehwa. Gary was now the third farmer to be caught up in the armed abduction of David Stevens.

Hyacinth kept on writing down what both Gary and Steve were saying: *The police say they know what is happening ... We've had to drop back a bit but are still following ...*

At exactly 3.00 pm the convoy of vehicles arrived at the crossroads leading into the dusty little nowhere town of Murewha. Hyacinth recorded the last words spoken by Steve Krynauw before radio communication was lost: *We're at the Mukarkate turn-off now ... we're almost in Murehwa ... They've gone over the crossroads ...*

With the noisy, static-laden radio communication suddenly lost, Hyacinth was bombarded by calls from people in the community. Everyone was frantic to know what was going on and what they could do to help.

Where are they now? ...
What's happened? ...
What are the guys planning to do? ...
The Murehwa police are still not showing any sign of moving ...

Hyacinth was as much in the dark as the rest of the community. She wrote: *3.06 pm: Lost signal. John and Steve calling on channel 7.Very distorted. Can't hear anything.*

While Hyacinth battled to keep up with the radio communications, the frantic calls and barrage of questions, the outside world began to get a hint that something was going on in Macheke. At 3.31 Hyacinth asked: *Is there any other news? The BBC are on the phone.*

John Osborne and Steve Krynauw arrived in Murehwa. It is a tiny town, and it was not hard to locate the three vehicles they had been following all afternoon. The car, Land Rover and minibus were all parked outside the war veterans' headquarters. This drab building, with its spacious yard behind, was known to Murehwa residents as a torture centre and Chenjerai Hunzvi's own ZEXCOM headquarters.

John and Steve drove past and then did a U-turn. Their progress was slow, as there was a mob of people, perhaps a hundred strong, milling around on the road outside the war veterans' building. Most of these people must have seen David Stevens, handcuffed and grossly outnumbered, being taken into the building minutes before. John and Steve drove back through the crowd and as they drew level with the building someone shot at them.

The situation had deteriorated drastically, and John instinctively increased his speed. Steve had radio communication with Gary Luke, who had just arrived in the town. *Get out now, Gary,* he called on the radio, *we're being shot at.* A hasty decision was needed when they saw that they were being followed by a white car. John locked his wheels and swung into the Murehwa police camp. The driver of the white car shot at them again, but did not turn into the police station.

Gary Luke prepared to turn his vehicle and leave immediately as Steve had instructed him, but it was too late. The mob was swarming towards him. Gary watched John and Steve drive past him and suddenly thirty or forty people were upon him, shouting, waving their fists, throwing stones at his car. All wearing T-shirts of the ruling party, they were an angry mob, out of control, unstoppable. The Macheke police, who had followed him into Murehwa, sat and watched but still did nothing.

Gary had no option but to follow John and Steve. He watched them turn into the police camp and saw them being shot at. He drove past and hid his car in a small patch of bush off the road, waiting for the crowd to disperse and the car with the gunman to leave. Moments later Gary also drove into the Murehwa police camp, seeking protection and refuge in what should have been the safest place in the world.

The farmers went into the Murehwa police station to officially report that David Stevens had been abducted by armed men, that he had been handcuffed and taken away in his own vehicle. They went in to try and find out what had happened to their friend, to try and get the police to go and help him. They went in to report that they had been shot at twice, minutes before, in broad daylight in the streets of Murehwa. They went in for protection, for refuge, for safety. John, Steve and Gary did what anyone in their right minds would have done; they sought help from the police. They had no one else to turn to; they were out of radio range and could not tell anyone else what was happening.

There were a number of policemen standing around in the sun outside the charge office and another half dozen inside. At this point, the Macheke police drove into the car park. Inside the charge office no one would speak to the farmers except to tell them to move into a courtyard behind because they were in the way. As the farmers began to do as they were told, David Stevens's Land Rover arrived in the car park. Ten men got out and immediately ransacked the vehicles belonging to John and Gary. In front of all the policemen standing around, the thugs stole everything movable and then deflated the tyres. Not a single policeman even tried to stop them.

John, Gary and Steve were told to stand in a corner of the enclosed courtyard behind the charge office. No one would speak to them; no one would listen to them or tell them what was going on. Two men appeared at a locked gate in the courtyard wall. One of them was armed with a .303 rifle. 'Open it!' he demanded of a nearby policeman. 'Open it!'

The policeman, one of perhaps twenty in the complex, unlocked the gate and stood aside as the armed man ordered the three farmers out. They had no choice but to comply, but as they passed the office of the Member in Charge, John tried one last time to get this madness stopped.

'Are you happy with this?' he asked, looking directly into the Member in Charge's eyes. The most senior police officer in the station did not answer; he turned his head away and did not say a single word.

The three farmers were frogmarched out of the courtyard and across the car park. They were forced into the back of David Stevens's Land Rover. Witnessing this were the Macheke police, men from their home town, officers the farmers knew by name. In front of all the Murehwa police, the three farmers were abducted from the police station. Several men got into the Land Rover with the three farmers, sitting on their laps so that they could not move. The Land Rover left what should have been the sanctity of the Murehwa police camp.

John, Steve and Gary had no way of contacting anyone or of telling the world they had just been abducted from a police station. They had no one to turn to for help and were completely alone, completely at the mercy of men calling themselves 'war veterans'.

Stuart Gemmill can see the main road that leads to Murehwa from his farmhouse. His home had become a gathering place for the anxious farmers from the Macheke district. On that fateful afternoon a number of Daisies and farmers were there, waiting to go and help the moment they were called. When Stuart began losing radio contact with John, Steve and Gary, he and five others set out along the road towards Murehwa in order to maintain radio contact. Along the road they met the Member in Charge of Macheke police. The farmers stopped and spoke to the inspector, who told them that there was nothing to worry about, the situation was under control and the four missing men were all in a meeting at the Murehwa police station.

The inspector told all the farmers to turn round and go back to their homes. The farmers discussed the matter amongst themselves for a few minutes. The most worrying aspect was the lack of radio communication with the four men who were supposedly safe and sound in Murehwa. It was decided that Stuart Gemmill and Ian Hardy would go on to assess the situation and try to renew radio contact so as to be able to report back to all the other farmers in the district. In Ian's pick-up truck, they headed for Murehwa.

Hyacinth recorded their messages as they came in. *Stuart says they are going there to find out what's going on ... They will relay back ... They've met the Macheke police on the road near the Rota turn-off ... The Member in Charge is in the vehicle. He says that Dave, John, Steve and Gary are in a meeting with the Murehwa Member in Charge ... The Macheke police say that everything is OK ...*

Arriving at the police camp in Murehwa, the first thing Stuart and Ian saw was the two vehicles belonging to their friends. They went into the police station and were directed to an office which had 'I/C Violence' stencilled on the door. A plain-clothes policeman asked them their names and addresses before telling them that their friends were in a meeting with the Member in Charge. They were also told not to go into Murehwa town as the situation was 'volatile'.

Ian and Stuart bought a cold drink in the police canteen and went back to the charge office. There another policeman spoke to them, telling them that the four missing farmers were in a meeting with the District Administrator. The messages were changing and getting confused, so Ian and Stuart went back out to the car park. They sat in Ian's car and relayed a radio message to Hyacinth through another radio link.

Hyacinth recorded the times and details of all the calls from Stuart and Ian. At 3.48 pm she had a comprehensive record: *John, Steve and Gary are all in a meeting with the police ... David Stevens is still missing ...*

At 4.00 pm she wrote: *Steve, John and Gary have now gone to a meeting at the DA's office ... David Stevens's vehicle still not seen ... There are a lot of police standing around in the camp ... The police are not armed ... All the tyres on John and Gary's vehicles are flat ...*

Sitting in the car park of the Murehwa police camp, Stuart and Ian had no way of knowing that their three friends had already been taken away at gunpoint. They had no way of knowing where David Stevens was or of finding out what was happening. The police had told them that everything was under control, but they could not leave, not before they knew that the others were safe. They sat in the car park for half an hour. When they saw David Stevens's beige Land Rover drive in, Stuart immediately relayed a radio message to Hyacinth.

At 4.30 pm Hyacinth wrote down the details of the last radio message that would be heard from any of the six Macheke farmers: *David's Land Rover is coming in to the police camp now ... We can't see Dave ... Stand-by ...*

David Stevens's Land Rover stopped directly behind Ian's truck and ten men got out. One carried a rifle. Stuart was talking on the radio but his transmission was cut short when he was ordered to get out of the vehicle. Stuart and Ian were pushed and shoved towards the Land Rover. Both men knew they were in deep trouble but could do nothing. The numerous policemen still standing around in the car park could have done something, but they did not; they stood and watched as the two young farmers were abducted.

'Give me your car keys,' one of the 'war veterans' ordered, and Ian complied. Stuart and Ian were forced into the Land Rover and tied together by the wrist. Overpowered, outnumbered and unable to move, they were driven out of the Murehwa police camp.

David Stevens, John Osborne, Gary Luke, Steve Krynauw, Ian Hardy and Stuart Gemmill were now completely beyond help. Hyacinth and almost all the Macheke, Virginia and Murehwa farmers waited. Nothing more was heard. At 4.50 pm Hyacinth wrote: *All contact lost ...*

John Osborne, Steve Krynauw and Gary Luke were only driven a short distance from the Murehwa police station. The vehicle stopped outside the war veterans' headquarters and there was considerable confusion, with a large number of people milling around. John was taken from the vehicle and pushed towards the building. Steve and Gary, still unable to move, were driven away.

John Osborne and David Stevens

The moment John Osborne was clear of the departing Land Rover, he was attacked from all sides. John had no idea why he had been singled out, where Steve and Gary were being taken, or where David Stevens was. He was assaulted by a crowd of people using sticks, fan belts, wire rods, fists and feet. Still outside the building and in clear daylight, John was beaten until he fell to the ground. His glasses were gone, his head was bleeding profusely and his chest was unbearably painful, so much so that he could barely walk and was struggling to breathe.

Someone pushed John to a tap and held his head under a stream of cold water before he was led into the building, where he was taken to a small room and shoved inside. David Stevens was in the room, handcuffed and being pushed around by two men. John was also handcuffed and the two farmers were left alone. There was no time for discussion, no time for planning or explanations. There was barely time to draw breath, as within minutes their captors were back and pushing them outside and into a small car.

John and David sat in the back seat of the car, a man on either side of them. A rough blanket was thrown over their heads and the vehicle moved off, at first on a smooth tar road and then onto the bumpy, meandering tracks that surround Murehwa, until they stopped opposite a large pool of water. John and Dave, still handcuffed, were removed from the car by a man carrying a single-barrelled shotgun and led 50 to 100 metres from the car. As they walked David told John how sorry he was that his friend had got involved, and wished him luck. He said he'd had a good life, thanked John for being such a good friend and said goodbye to him. A second vehicle arrived and a lot more people got out.

John and David, unarmed, outnumbered, unable to defend themselves and with their wrists handcuffed, were both assaulted from all sides. Anything and everything was used as a weapon: fists and feet, sticks, stones, fan belts and wire rods. When John could barely stand or breathe, he was led away from the crowd and put back in the vehicle with two people guarding him, a man and a woman. He could hear the mob still beating David but could do nothing. The crowd went quiet, parted and a shot rang out. And then another. David Stevens was dead.

Someone in the crowd called for John to be brought from the vehicle.

'He's all right, he's Mr Bluegums,' another called.

'Yes, he's Mr Bluegums, he's all right,' someone else agreed.

Those two short sentences saved John Osborne's life.

There was confusion, whispered conversation, argument. Someone asked John where he wanted to be taken. John realised immediately that these people did not know what to do next. He thought of the only person he knew in Murehwa who might be able to help, a man he had met briefly, but who might be able to help. He asked to be taken there. There was more whispering, more confusion, and then a man approached, leaned into the car and said: 'Sorry for that.'

What the statement referred to was a mystery. Was it an apology for beating, for torture, for abduction, for murder? John, unable to see without his glasses, covered in bruises and lacerations, with excruciating pain in his chest, was taken, still handcuffed, to the home of the man he knew in Murehwa.

No one made a huge fuss of John Osborne as he sat, dazed and confused, in the home of his acquaintance in Murehwa. No one called for an ambulance or a doctor or the police. No one even tried to remove the handcuffs still shackling his wrists. Someone cleaned the blood from his face and smeared antiseptic over his hugely swollen black eye. Time passed slowly and confusion reigned. Some time later he was given a cup of tea and a stream of people wandered in, stared and whispered, wandered out. Someone came and removed the handcuffs, but still there was no urgency, no move to take him to hospital.

As evening drew in the police came, looked and left. Then other government officials came, looked and left. John barely spoke; he did not tell anyone what had happened, what he had witnessed – this was neither the time nor the place. He just sat and waited for sanity to return. It was completely dark when the police came back again. Trained, professional and experienced policemen asked John Osborne where he wanted to be taken. They did not take the initiative or offer alternatives; they did not take control of the situation. John, struggling to breathe, exhausted and in considerable pain, asked to be taken to hospital. The policemen did not help: they just left him where he was and departed again.

John was finally delivered by his acquaintance to the Murehwa police station – the same police station where his nightmare had begun that same day, a lifetime ago. He was put into a police Land Rover and taken to Borradaile hospital in Marondera. At 10.00 pm he was finally put into a hospital bed. He was covered in bruises and lacerations on his legs, arms, head, back and chest; he had five broken ribs and a punctured lung.

John Osborne was the first deeply traumatised survivor to emerge from the granite hills of Murehwa, the first man to tell the world that David Stevens was dead.

Steve Krynauw and Gary Luke
In the back of David Stevens's Land Rover, with men sitting on their

laps, Steve and Gary could do nothing but watch helplessly as the vehicle drew away from the war veterans' building and headed onto the dirt roads behind Murehwa. The verbal abuse was continuous.

'You are going to die.'

'You are stupid MDC supporters.'

'You are MDC and are going to die.'

'You are going to die.'

The abuse went on and on, sometimes in English, sometimes in Shona, mostly shouted, littered with political references, accusations and rhetoric.

Steve and Gary were relieved of all their possessions as the journey continued. Gary had his watch and wedding ring taken, then the Saint Christopher medal and chain from around his neck, finally his diary, pen, money, car keys and even his shoes. Steve had his watch taken, then his diary, pen, calculator, hat and car keys. For both men the loss of their possessions was not as important as the sentimental value attached to the items: a watch given by a deceased father, a hat that had been a Christmas present, a key ring that was a gift from a friend. Neither of the men could do anything as they were stripped of these parts of their lives.

Moments after the 'war veterans' had found and removed Steve's car keys, they felt something else in his pocket.

'There is still something in your pocket!' the man sitting on Steve's lap exclaimed.

Steve had 12 bullets in his pocket. He was licensed to carry a gun because he was a security officer; the police knew that he always carried a gun. When the man sitting on his lap discovered the bullets, however, the farmer was in deep trouble. His shirt was ripped open, exposing the handgun in its holster.

'Chef!' the war veteran shouted out. That one word, a very well-known Mozambican word, meaning the top person, the man in charge, immediately attracted the attention of everyone in the vehicle. Blows were rained on Steve from every direction as the Land Rover drew to a halt.

'Why have you got a gun?'

'We are going to kill you.'

'Now you are going to die.'

Steve tried to explain, to shield himself from the blows, the fists and feet that lashed out at him. Someone in the front of the vehicle aimed a gun at him and he was sure that he was going to be killed at that moment. Gary, with a gun pointed at his head, could do nothing. Steve was dragged out of the vehicle, kicked, punched and whipped with fan belts. He lost consciousness when a large rock was smashed into the right side of his face.

'We are going to kill you,' the men repeatedly screamed as they turned their attention to Gary, punching, kicking and hitting him. Gary remained conscious while he was assaulted. His assailants were youngsters, perhaps in their twenties, who were barely old enough to be men, let alone veterans of a war that had ended two decades before. Steve's unconscious body was thrown back into the vehicle and Gary immediately bent down to check his friend, to see if he was breathing, if he was alive. He gently moved Steve's head into an easier position to aid his breathing.

'Take that holster off him,' one of the youngsters spat at Gary, and he struggled with shaking, sticky fingers to untie the leather thongs holding Steve's shoulder holster together. He watched dazed and helpless as Steve drifted in and out of consciousness, watched helplessly as the men kicked and prodded Steve again and again as the vehicle wound deeper and deeper into the Murehwa hills.

Finally the Land Rover drew to a stop and Gary was pulled out, his hands bound together tightly with nylon rope. While Steve lay unconscious in the vehicle, Gary was pushed into the bush behind an outcrop of rocks on a granite kopje. Gary tried to defend himself, he kicked and flailed, but there were too many of them and they beat him with iron bars until he fell unconscious to the ground.

Steve does not remember being removed from the vehicle, nor does he remember much of the beating that followed. Neither man knows how long they lay unconscious, bound and bleeding on the Murehwa rocks. When they came round, they could not see their assailants. Steve suggested they try and escape but Gary was too weak; he could barely stand – and their attackers had not finished with them yet.

Gary and Steve were led back down the track to a waiting vehicle, this time not the Land Rover but a Toyota pick-up truck. They pleaded for their hands to be untied; the nylon rope was so tight that it was cutting off all feeling and circulation. The rope around Steve's wrists was loosened slightly before he was made to lie on his back in the truck. Gary was made to lie face down next to Steve, and a body was thrown on top of them.

'Move and you die,' someone declared.

Neither Steve nor Gary knew whose body lay on top of them, shielding them from the dark, the cold and the rain. Both men hovered on the edge of consciousness and life as the vehicle carried them off into the night.

At some time in the night the Toyota drew to a halt on a low bridge. The abductors got out and slashed all the tyres.

'Move and we kill you' they declared again, and then left.

Steve and Gary did not move, not until they were sure they were alone. Their nightmare had been going on for so long that they could not believe that perhaps it was finally over. Neither of them knew what time it was, how far away dawn was. It took them a long time, but they finally managed to untie the ropes binding each other's hands. They moved the body off them and got out of the truck. Steve's immediate thought was to get as far away as possible from both the vehicle and the area. He suggested they escape immediately, but Gary had to hold on to the side of the truck to stop himself from falling over. He was dizzy and disorientated and could barely walk. The two farmers got into the cab of the vehicle. There was a farm radio, but the microphone had been ripped out. They rested and tried to recover some strength, drifting in and out of sleep and consciousness until the blackness of night began to fade.

As soon as it was light enough to get their bearings, Steve and Gary got out of the Toyota. They looked at the body in the back, saw that it was David Stevens and knew that there was nothing they could do, knew they did not have the strength to carry him. Barefoot, they headed south, following the dusty animal trails through the sparsely vegetated land towards civilisation. It was a slow and painful walk; they were drained, exhausted and in deep shock. It took them perhaps four hours to go five kilometres, but at 8.00 am they arrived at the first farm on the edge of the communal lands. The farm was deserted, the entire district having been evacuated the afternoon before, but Gary and Steve were let in by a worker. They were given coffee, jackets and spare keys to the farmer's vehicle, and they headed towards Macheke, towards home.

Steve and Gary went to the nearest inhabited farm, where they were met by six farmers who carried them to a vehicle waiting to take them to hospital. At Borradaile hospital in Marondera they were met by a battery of reporters who wanted to hear of this horrific ordeal, which had gone on for more than eighteen hours.

Steve Krynauw had a fractured right cheekbone, a black right eye and lumps all over his head, face and jaw. All his top teeth were loose, his mouth, nose and lips were severely swollen and he had widespread bruising on his back, stomach and chest.

Gary Luke had a six-inch cut and a depressed fracture of his forehead. He had another four-inch cut and fracture of the skull behind his right ear. He had two black eyes, swollen nose, mouth and lips and severe bruising on his arms, shoulders and legs.

Ian Hardy and Stuart Gemmill

Ian Hardy and Stuart Gemmill, overpowered, outnumbered and with their hands tied, were taken from the police station in David Stevens's Land Rover to the same building where all the other farmers had been, the war veterans' headquarters. The yard was full of people wearing T-shirts and caps that advertised the ruling party. The two farmers were forced and pushed through the crowd to the back of the complex. There was a lot of noise, talking and shouting and people pulled at Ian's hair as he passed by. Through all the noise and madness Ian heard one voice: 'Out!' came an authoritative order in English. 'They will see too much,' the man added, this time in Shona.

Ian and Stuart were pushed and shoved back through the crowd and into the Land Rover. They were driven a fairly short distance on a dirt road and the vehicle stopped at the base of a granite hill. Ian and Stuart were ordered out and were hit in the face and on the backs of their legs. They had their shoes and watches removed and were then ordered to climb up the hill. As the two young farmers walked, their hands still roped together, some men whipped at their legs and backs with a sjambok while others punched and slapped them. Stuart was sure they were being taken to their own execution and his fears increased as they were pushed into a cave.

Inside the cave, Ian and Stuart were made to sit on the ground while a man performed some sort of a ritual over and around them. Was it a ritual to appease the spirits in advance, perhaps? Stuart, now convinced he was about to be killed, began to prepare himself for the end. Then the questions began, questions punctuated with slaps, punches and kicks.

'Who is MDC in your area?'

'Who is the head of MDC in Macheke?'

A man grabbed Stuart's right ear and held a knife to it, threatened to cut it off and use it to do cave paintings with.

'What materials have they got for the MDC? T-shirts, cards?'

'Where do all the MDC people in Macheke live? Who are they?'

It didn't matter what answers Ian and Stuart gave to the questions, still they were beaten.

'Do you whites want to rule Zimbabwe again?' one man demanded. 'Why don't you go back to Britain where you came from?'

Stuart and Ian, until now shackled to each other, had their hands untied and then re-tied separately behind their backs. They then had their feet tied together with webbing and were made to lie face down on the ground in the cave. The questions continued and the beatings intensified. Both men were whipped with long sticks and a sjambok made of heavy tyre treading. They were beaten with wooden poles on their backs, legs and calves. Stuart was slashed with a hot knife on his back and Ian was burnt with glowing cigarette ends on his back. They were beaten on the soles of their feet repeatedly with a rubber baton and then rolled over onto their backs. The questions continued.

'Why do you want to change the government?'

'Who is MDC?'

'Why don't you go back to Britain?'

Both Ian and Stuart were beaten on the knees by a man wielding an iron bar and were then told to roll over again.

'We are going to shoot you,' someone said and a weapon appeared.

Stuart rolled over. In his mind, he said goodbye to his wife, and waited for the bullet. It did not come; perhaps the gun had jammed, perhaps the 'war veterans' changed their minds – but suddenly it was over. It was dark now and the men started to leave.

'We will be back later for your *machendis* [genitals],' one man said as he left.

When Ian and Stuart were sure their assailants had gone, they called out to each other, and managed to wriggle close enough to untie each other's hands. They knew they had to get out of the cave, out of sight and as far away as they possibly could. Their progress was slow, agonisingly slow, but the two young farmers managed to get away from the cave. Neither could walk because of the repeated whippings inflicted on the soles of their feet, so they crawled as far away as they could, into the deepest bush they could find.

They wanted to try and get down to the main Murehwa/Harare road that night, but their injuries were far too severe, so they hid in the dense bush and waited for dawn and for their strength to return. At least twice during the night their attackers returned and seemed to be looking for them. It had rained on and off during the night, though, erasing their tracks. About an hour before dawn a vehicle arrived and they heard people walking around, searching. More vehicles arrived, and Stuart heard a man speaking in Shona: 'Dispol [District Police] says after yesterday's mix-up, you must leave these people alone and return the bag of kit.'

It was probable that the people searching for them now were either police or had some police authority, but the farmers did not dare to call out. The 'bag of kit' referred to was possibly the gun they had been threatened with in the cave the night before. When Ian and Stuart heard the people and vehicles leaving, they crawled out of their hiding place and into the sun to get warm. They found a puddle of water in the rocks and drank from it and then waited out in the open so that they could be seen by rescuers.

Some time in the middle of the morning an army helicopter appeared, hovered over the two men and then left. Forty-five minutes later a small fixed-wing aircraft flew overhead and also disappeared. At about midday a local man approached Ian and Stuart and offered to help them down to the main road. The farmers did not know who to trust any more, so they declined and waited until a short time later when a number of armed Police Support Unit members arrived in two Land Rovers. Under the supervision of an inspector from the Marondera police, Ian and Stuart were carried down to the vehicles and taken to Murehwa police station, where they were transferred to other vehicles and transported to Marondera.

Ian Hardy and Stuart Gemmill arrived at Borradaile hospital in Marondera a few minutes after 3.00 pm on Sunday, 16 April 2000 –

the last two men to be rescued from the granite hills of Murehwa. They were lucky to be alive, immensely relieved to be safe.

Ian Hardy had extensive bruising and deep bleeding under the skin on his face, head, arms, chest, back, legs and soles of his feet. Ian had lacerations on his scalp, calves, thighs, arms, and chest. He had a black eye, swollen nose, lips and mouth and cigarette burns on his buttocks.

Stuart Gemmill had a broken tooth, a fractured thumb and a broken bone in his left hand. He had extensive bruising and deep bleeding under the skin on his face, back, buttocks legs, arms and the soles of his feet. He had lacerations on his scalp, back, legs and feet.

THREE

HEARTS OF STONE

T he story of what had happened that weekend in Murehwa was so brutal and gruesome that, both for myself and for others who had been tortured, I felt I had to know what had become of the survivors. So few of the people who have been tortured and suffered the foulest of abuses in Zimbabwe have been able to speak out; unable to tell their stories, instead they must live with their private agony. Many of them may never tell what happened to them in the hellish years of Zimbabwe's political madness.

One year and eight days after those five men were abducted from a police station in Zimbabwe, beaten to a pulp and left for dead, I set out to meet them, to find out how the anniversary of their weekend from hell had been. I had absolutely no idea what to expect. I had no idea how people survive the horrendous beatings and terror these five men had experienced. It was beyond comprehension that not one single person had been arrested in connection with these crimes. Even more amazing, however, was that these men were not only still in Zimbabwe, but still on their farms, still farming, still living in the same community where their nightmare had taken place.

The commitment of these men to their country, to Zimbabweans, to agriculture and to their neighbourhood was awe-inspiring. I felt humbled as I met and listened to each of them. More than humility, though, I felt a great sense of honour that people of this calibre would be a part of the new Zimbabwe.

On a beautiful autumn morning I travelled down the red dust roads that traverse the Macheke farming area and, as I had a million times in the last year, I found myself filled with an overwhelming sense of disbelief. How was it possible that communities such as this one could have been reduced to such a state of chaos in so short a time? Once lush fields abutting the road were now mostly bare, weed-infested and untended. For political gain, to win votes, under the guise of giving land to the people, our government had allowed all these food-growing fields to be taken over by handfuls of squatters. Squatters who called themselves 'war veterans'; squatters in their early twenties who could not possibly have been veterans of a war finished two decades before. Squatters whose main preoccupation seemed to be to scare, intimidate, harass and threaten the legal owners. Squatters who apparently had no desire to get out there and tend the fields, grow the food needed for thirteen million Zimbabweans. Squatters who had planted handfuls of maize in the middle of vast fields, maize which would not even feed their families for a month, let alone an entire nation for a year. What shame I felt – and what utter disgust.

For a fortnight in the year 2000, the names of the five Zimbabwean farmers had been on everyone's lips, their faces in every newspaper, on every television news channel, on dozens of Internet web sites. Barely a year later, the world had forgotten. The physical scars of the beatings these men had endured in Murehwa were virtually gone and I wondered now why any of them had agreed to see me, why any of them would want to remember such horror. But like me they wanted the truth to be told, they wanted the world to see the cold, brutal facts in print, they wanted people to know what had really gone on in Murehwa, and why. These men did not want the sensational one-liners in newspapers; they did not want their bloodied faces and bruised backs on the front of magazines, they did not want the fabrication that had surrounded almost every media report, they just wanted the plain facts and absolute truths to be told.

My first meeting was with Ian Hardy and his wife Marjo. Ian was a farm manager and looked like any other strong, healthy 35-year-old. I was not surprised by all the security measures on the farm; the high security fence topped with barbed wire, the locked gates, the dogs, the hand-held farm radio, the cell phones. All of these things had become the norm on every Zimbabwean farm. Being prepared and ready for the worst, for marauding 'war veterans', for eviction, for flight – all of these had become a terrifying part of everyday life.

Throughout our meeting both Ian and Marjo wore dark, mirrored sunglasses. Perhaps they had had enough of staring eyes and prying questions, but they welcomed me, answered my questions. The meeting was tense and awkward, perhaps because they didn't know if they could trust me. So many reporters had come and gone in the last year. So many strangers had pointed their microphones and cameras at Ian and Marjo but none, said Ian, had really told the true story, none had told what really happened in Murehwa. All the reporters had looked for headline angles – and that in itself defied belief, because there was more than enough sensational horror in the truth. When Marjo handed me copies of Ian's statement, the hospital reports, the radio transmission records and the photographs of Ian's injuries, I was overwhelmed.

I looked at the words on Ian's medical records. 'Severe assault ... blunt trauma ... deep haematoma ... linear abrasions ... lacerations ... cigarette burns ...' And the description of Ian's back: 'Covered from top to bottom in large haematomas and numerous linear abrasions.' None of these words could prepare me, as a layman, for the photographs of Ian Hardy. Even the dictionary telling me that a 'haematoma' is a 'solid swelling of clotted blood' could not prepare me. Ian's back, buttocks and legs were almost completely black with bruising; they were a mass of subcutaneous bleeding, a solid, obscene mass. His face was so swollen as to make him almost unrecognisable; his eye, ear, lips, nose and chin were covered in purple bruising and dry blood. The anguish on Ian's face as he lay naked in a hospital bed was clear, horrendous and palpable.

Looking at the photographs of Ian Hardy later I could not stem my tears. I could hear the dull thudding of rubber batons hitting the soles of his feet, the whistle of wind against whips and sticks before they slammed into his back, I could feel Ian cringing. I could feel his heart thumping, hear the rushing and hissing roar in his ears, taste the blood in his mouth. Worst, though, I could feel his desperate need to cover his head, to try and shield himself from the blows, to try and roll himself up into a foetal position, an instinctive and basic need he could not fulfil because his hands were tied behind his back.

Ian Hardy knew that what happened to him was motivated by politics and not by a need for land. He knew too that David Stevens was not murdered because he was white or a farmer. David Stevens was murdered because of his involvement in the Rural Council, because he had uncovered massive corruption and was about to expose it. Ian told me that David Stevens was a very good man, that he was greatly liked in the community and worked tirelessly to help his peasant neighbours and his workers and to improve the facilities in the district.

David Stevens was murdered for political reasons only. Not only was he an active supporter of the MDC, he was a man who was determined to expose corruption and fraud. David, according to his widow Maria, 'oozed goodness' and that was why he was such a threat to the ruling party. He could not be bought, blackmailed, bribed or persuaded to keep quiet. He was a man of principle and the ruling party needed him permanently silenced.

Ian Hardy went to try and help David Stevens because he wanted to. He chose to be a good human being, to try and help his neighbour. Now he and Marjo wanted to leave all the painful memories behind, to forget and move on. When I met them they were preparing to leave the country. They also wanted answers, though. They wanted to know if the policemen who witnessed the abduction of farmers from a police station would be prosecuted for dereliction of duty. They wanted to know who was responsible for the abductions and the beatings. They wanted to know if these criminals would ever be apprehended, prosecuted and sentenced. They were not alone in their questions or in their desire that justice be done.

Stuart Gemmill was with Ian Hardy in the Murehwa caves. He too had committed no crime when he was abducted from a police station and beaten almost to death. Stuart is thirty, slightly built and still living on and working his farm in Macheke. He was waiting for me outside the electrified fence that surrounded his simple but beautiful prefabricated wooden farmhouse. The gates were always kept locked, the fence always charged, the dogs always on guard. We sat at a small table on the veranda of Stuart's home and looked out onto the lands into which he has invested his life. The tea flowed as freely as the jokes and I was struck by the intense life and humour of this tall, lithe and deeply tanned young farmer.

Stuart's property, like three-quarters of Zimbabwe's farms, has been designated for compulsory acquisition by the Zimbabwe government. He has received the Section 8 letter from the Minister of Agriculture informing him that his land is to be taken, that everything he has worked his entire life for is to be 'acquired' without any compensation. Stuart has legally contested the designation of his farm, his life, but for now that means nothing. A handful of 'war veterans' and squatters have occupied his farm for well over a year; they have built small shacks and they sit, day after day after day. They do not farm, they do not toil under the hot African sun; they just sit and watch, watch and wait.

Like me, Stuart is a born and raised Zimbabwean and like me, he is white. He is a farmer and he has lost all his rights in the country of his birth. Stuart is an honest, open and forthright man and there are many times during our conversation when his eyes unashamedly fill with tears. He does not try to turn away from me, he conceals nothing, his voice is sincere, his words genuine.

During the assault in Murehwa, Stuart believes that he came into direct contact with blood from the hands of one of his attackers. He underwent a course of antiretroviral drugs to ensure that Aids would not be a possibility, a course that spanned months and had appalling side effects. These drugs and side effects were something Stuart was determined to endure; he and his young wife, Lise, have no children yet but it is something they look forward to in the future. For weeks on end Stuart was tired and lethargic and the days drifted by in a haze of sleep and nausea.

Emerging from the course of drugs, Stuart was nervous and on edge with many flashbacks of the horrors he had survived. In counselling sessions he told it all, re-lived the horrors and by so doing, managed to put the nightmare behind him. He talked openly to me about how he had felt during the attack. How there were moments when he gave up hope, when he was desperate for it to be over. How he had been so convinced that he was going to die, that he was going to be shot. Stuart's eyes filled with tears as he told me that the hardest part of looking at his own death was having to say goodbye to Lise in his mind.

Being so close to death has strengthened his marriage, his life and his convictions. Stuart talked about how he had felt when he and Ian finally managed to crawl out of the Murehwa caves when their attackers left. How he had felt an enormous sense of both relief and hope. For Stuart at that moment there was almost a sense of satisfaction, 'a case of you haven't won', he told me, his deep and intense eyes shining. 'Facing death has made me stronger,' he said.

A year after the attack Stuart was strong and felt very positive about both his future and his place in Zimbabwe. The anniversary of the abduction and assault in Murehwa was a day when Stuart had faced the last of his horrors. He had stayed at home on his farm, 'to be able to say it was OK and to put the demons to rest'.

Nothing happened on that day, it was like any other day and that in itself gave Stuart strength and hope for the future. Like so many of us now, Stuart spoke from the heart, with depth and patriotic fervour.

'This is my home,' he said, 'I want to grow old here.'

Gary Luke is 45 and the only one of the five abducted farmers who still has visible reminders and is still undergoing medical treatment as a result of the assault in Murehwa. When I met Gary he was still on his farm, still working the land, still putting in crops to support Zimbabwe. His farm is listed for compulsory acquisition by the government of Zimbabwe and he has been served with a Section 5 notice of intention of seizure without compensation. Like Stuart Gemmill, Gary Luke was legally contesting the acquisition of his property, demanding his constitutional rights as a Zimbabwean. Gary makes his living from tobacco and when I visited him the lands were ploughed and prepared, ready for another crop. Gary was not sure if the handful of 'war veterans' currently squatting on his land would allow him to put in this next crop, but he was prepared.

Gary and his wife Jenny were very welcoming and we sat out on the veranda of their home below the beautiful Macheke hills. Gary was very reluctant to answer specific questions about what had happened in Murehwa. He said that he had told the story dozens of times to scores of reporters and that it 'had been done to death, and was wrong every time'. I knew exactly how this misrepresentation felt and told Gary how I too had entertained journalists, told them everything and then been shocked and angered when I read their printed copy which was often a complete fabrication. We all laughed when I told how a British journalist had described my gum tree plantations as 'lush orchards'. Perhaps it was because I did actually know what it was like to have my privacy, my home and my farm filled with journalists and cameras, that Gary did answer my questions.

Gary gave me a copy of the statement he had made after his abduction and assault. Like the others, he was convinced that David Stevens did not die because of his colour or profession, but for his political beliefs. A year after his experience in Murehwa, Gary had not given in or given up. His life's work, assets and all his capital lay in the lands around his home and he remained totally committed to both his farm and his neighbourhood.

Gary continues to do 'Godfather' duty and actively takes part in the farming association. He is convinced that the closeness, unity and organisation of the district has saved many lives, and listening to their daily radio communications, I am sure he is right. Gary's torture at the hands of 'war veterans' in Murehwa made him more aware than most of man's mortality. 'It made me realise,' he said, 'how slender the link is between being alive and dead.'

As we talked I could not help but look at the vivid scar that sections Gary's forehead, from his eyebrows to his hairline. The scar crosses a deep and noticeable hollow in his skull. Medically it is called a depressed fracture; in reality, though, it is a daily and very visible reminder of being tied up and beaten again and again. Gary's powerful and stocky physique cannot disguise the pain in his eyes or the tired resignation in his voice.

At the time of our meeting Gary had had three operations on his forehead. In the first operation, surgeons found scarring on his brain and had to stitch the dura, the tough membrane that covers the brain, before they could deal with the surface lacerations. Doctors told Gary that the thickness of the bone on his forehead was now only a third of what it should be and that further operations would be needed to increase the bone density in order to adequately protect his brain. Before this could happen, though, his other injuries had to be attended to. He needed 40 stitches to other lacerations on his body, including behind his right ear where another fracture was found. Gary has a 40 per cent loss of hearing to his right ear and his vision has also been affected.

Once the bruising and swelling all over Gary's body had subsided and stitches had been removed, he went back into hospital for the first operation to rebuild the bone on his forehead. Bone was removed from his right hip and inserted in his forehead. This new bone was soon reabsorbed by his body and another operation was necessary. This time, bone was removed from Gary's left hip to be grafted into his forehead. When I met him many months later the bone had again been largely reabsorbed, but Gary had had enough. He is scarred for life.

Gary's wife, Jenny, was on the farm when her husband went to Murehwa to try and help David Stevens. For Jenny, there was a multitude of emotions: fear for her husband, not knowing what was going on or where he was, not being able to speak to him and, worst of all, being told to evacuate. When the farmers were abducted from the police station in Murehwa, the entire Macheke neighbourhood had been ordered to evacuate their farms. Seventy farmers, in less than two hours, were told by the farmers running the area's security to get out of their homes. There was no time to make plans, to pack or decide on what valuables should be taken. They were told to get off their farms before dark – and 70 farmers and their families did exactly that. Jenny Luke, not knowing where her husband was or what was happening, had followed orders – she had her teenage son to think of.

Jenny stayed with friends in Harare, but her memory of that night is of incessant phone calls and desperate messages to try and find out where her husband was. Jenny phoned the Murehwa police station seven times that night. Each time she was told something different; no one would tell her the truth. She could do absolutely nothing.

Like so many Zimbabwean farmers who have had to vacate their homes in a few short hours, Jenny no longer has to look at her life to decide on the priorities, she knows them instinctively. 'Possessions are absolutely nothing,' she says, and having experienced it myself, I know that she is right. Coming out of Zimbabwe's farm invasions with your life and the people you love is the only thing of any real importance. Jenny, like so many other Zimbabwean women, has found her real self, has discovered her inner strengths and is at peace with herself and her family.

Steve Krynauw is 54, has four grown children and has recently become a grandfather. He was the oldest of the five men abducted and beaten in Murehwa and the encounter has perhaps affected him more deeply than the others. Steve is thin and lean, his face almost gaunt, and his deep-set eyes often filled with tears as he told me what he could remember of the events that took place in Murehwa.

Because Steve had a gun, he was knocked unconscious almost as soon as the weapon was discovered and his memory of the events was scant and quite disjointed. As I pieced the story together for him from five different versions, Steve was often very surprised at what he heard. He realised how much he didn't know, how much more had been happening as he drifted in and out of consciousness. Steve thinks that perhaps if he went back to Murehwa, back to where it started, he might remember more. 'I might get back some of the missing pieces, although I'm not sure if I want that.'

Even after a year it was incredibly hard to forget and come to terms with what had happened. One of the things Steve remembers clearly is the feeling of being so totally outnumbered when he, Gary and John were taken to the Murehwa war veterans' building. 'I have a very clear outside picture of the three of us getting out of the Land Rover and walking to the building. Three little white boys, very dejected, out of our depth and the focused target of hundreds of people's hatred. I can see us from outside very clearly; our body language must have been pathetic. When they said they only wanted the first person and the two of us walked back to the Land Rover it was almost like going back to a haven.'

Steve, in common with all the other men, said that fear was not really a big factor during the ordeal. 'There were flashes of fear, but it didn't last, it didn't seem to be a necessary or helpful emotion.'

Steve is no longer on his Macheke farm. It too has been designated for compulsory acquisition by the Zimbabwe government, occupied by war veterans and squatters and served with Section 7 and 8 notices of designation. Whilst Steve's farm was no longer a viable enterprise for him, he was still in the district and working as security liaison between farmers and the police. The bulk of Steve's job is done on the farm radio, cell phone and telephone and he is on call 24 hours a day, seven days a week. On some days there is not much happening and on others the demands are incessant as farmers call on him for help. It is indeed ironic that a man who was abducted from a police station should now spend his days trying to get the police to help other farmers in trouble. Steve knows that the police in Murehwa should have intervened when he and the others were being abducted, but he understands, as we all do, that they are bound by the orders of their superiors. Superiors who have openly and publicly admitted that they support the ruling party and take their orders from top government ministers.

Steve is convinced that law and order will return, that sanity will be restored to the farms, and is committed to seeing it through to the end. When that point arrives, he knows that he will no longer have a job or an income and that his farm will belong to the government. His future is insecure, unclear and very worrying. As with all of us, Steve had invested his life in his farm and had intended to see out his days there. However, he is both positive and strong, knowing that although his life will never be the same again, new doors will open. He has no intention of leaving Zimbabwe.

John Osborne, a born and bred Zimbabwean, is a tall and lean 50-year-old, married, with two young teenage children. He is well known and greatly respected in the community and speaks the local language fluently. A very active farmer, he grows wheat and tobacco and is involved in many community projects. John was the only one of the farmers who saw David Stevens alive and spoke to him after he had been abducted from his farm. Calmly, he told me what had happened to him in Murehwa.

As with all the farmers, John Osborne's return to physical and mental health had not been easy. John is a thoughtful and astute man and he knew that dealing with the realities of his ordeal were not something he could do alone. He had seen things that the mind refuses to accept. He went for professional counselling, which helped him come to terms with the horrors of what he had seen and experienced.

John accepts, though, that much of what happened, or didn't happen, will remain a mystery. He does not know why he was removed from the Land Rover in Murehwa town, why he was not killed and why his abductors took him back to the town after the murder of David Stevens. These are questions that John will never have answers to and he has to accept that reality too.

Looking death in the face, realising your own mortality, is something that all of the men had to face that weekend in Murehwa. When, a year before, I had had a youngster threaten to kill me on my farm, I thought I knew what death looked like. I thought I knew how it felt to face my own mortality. But as I listened to each of these men tell me how it had felt for them, I was not sure any more if I did in fact know. Perhaps it was because they had been beaten, whipped and kicked and had faced extreme physical pain that their emotions were so different from what mine had been. John Osborne tried to put his thoughts and feelings into words for me. 'I do now realise that after a good hiding and the immediate prospect of dying, how much shock and adrenalin take over. It's almost as though there are no secrets left about dying. Pain is there ... but time seems to pass so quickly and dying is just another step. I don't feel scared of dying any more.'

John is very close to his wife and children and his feelings for them are the one emotion he remembers clearly when he thought he was going to die in Murehwa. 'I remember feeling extreme regret that I wouldn't see my family again. It was an overpowering feeling.'

John's love for and commitment to his family is very strong; so is his belief that he has a place and a future in Zimbabwe. He wants to be a farmer, wants to have a place and a role in the country of his birth. John, like so many other white Zimbabwean farmers, sees that the land imbalances are very real and believes that there are ways of legitimately and legally correcting them. John though, has not allowed himself to be taken in by the propaganda force-fed to Zimbabweans by the politicians. He is a widely read man, well informed and in no doubt at all that it is politics and votes behind the farm invasions, not land. He also sees the differences and conflicts that inevitably exist in a country containing two such diverse cultures.

During the early stages of the invasion of farms, John was often called on to help his neighbours negotiate with hostile and aggressive men who stood shouting and banging on farm gates. John's fluency in the local language, his understanding of the cultural courtesies, often made him the best person for farmers to call on for help. John described so well the scene he has witnessed at many farm gates. In one such encounter: 'What struck me then was the body language of the two whites, both had thunderous looks on their faces. One had his arms crossed and was rocking back and forth with his weight on one leg, the youngster had his hands on his hips. Both classic confrontation stances.'

As outsider and negotiator, however, John saw the classic stances from both sides and his description was chillingly accurate. Even though it was wrapped in humour, it put a human face onto what was the most desperate situation. He told me how he was called to negotiate at a farm gate. On his way there he saw a dog that undoubtedly had rabies. The creature was thin, mangy, infested with ticks and trotting determinedly in a straight line. John was urgently needed on the squatted farm next door, so he called on his farm radio for someone to come out and shoot the dog. Arriving at the newly invaded farm, outside the locked gates, John began the process of working out who was leading the 70-strong band of invaders, who it was he should try and talk to in order to calm the situation down.

On the inside of the locked gates were two white farmers; their dogs were locked inside, the situation was tense. John relates, 'Some fellow, obviously a war veteran, by his dress and attitude, came over obviously highly annoyed about something. "You tell that white I was bitten by his dog," he shouted at me.

'I looked at my neighbour, I knew his dogs were inside the fence. Realisation dawned.

' "*Shamwari* [friend], the white only has two dogs and they are both locked up."

' "I don't care, it was his dog. It has bitten me."

' "Was this dog a thin animal with a white blaze on its chest?"

' "Ya, you see, you know it, that's the one it has bitten me."'

The argument was interrupted at that moment when John's wife called on the radio. The thin dog John had seen earlier had been found and shot and there was no doubt that the animal had been rabid. John knew that it was this dog that had bitten the war veteran and he needed to impart the information immediately to the man. By now though the war veteran was adopting his own 'confrontational stance'. This time he pulled off his shirt.

'Look, this is where that white's dog has bitten me.'

Right up on his chest, just below his chin was a large bite mark. John told the man it was very probable that he had been bitten by the rabid dog. The man stared at him aggressively at first but suddenly seemed to understand the seriousness of his own predicament. He started to become agitated and the stare dropped.

'You mean rabies? That disease kills doesn't it?'

'It certainly does, it's deadly serious and you had better go and get an injection.'

'Aaah, shit!' the war veteran mumbled. He fumbled and shuffled for a moment before asking John if he could give him a lift to the nearest clinic. John politely pointed out that 70 people were screaming the odds at a farm gate, making outrageous demands, and that calming this situation was his first priority. The war veteran, perhaps in fact the man who had instigated the farm invasion, left rapidly in the direction of the clinic and was not seen again.

For me, John's story about the war veteran and the rabid dog said it all about Zimbabwe's land invasions. People do have to find ways to work out the past imbalances; they also have to accept the truths that are all around them and agree that nothing is ever what it seems at first glance.

Meeting and talking to the five farmers who went to Murehwa to try and save David Stevens was a very traumatic experience for me. There were a multitude of emotions and many sleepless or nightmare-filled nights as I lived through their horrors. It took me more than two months to be able to sit down calmly and re-tell their story. As I did, though, I realised how incredibly special all of these five men were. There was no hate or anger, or even a desire for revenge. Instead there was love and humour and light. There was a determination to stand up for what is right, an understanding of horror, an acceptance of mortality. And, most incredibly, a very strong patriotism combined with a desire to remain in Zimbabwe and a belief that it would all come right one day. I would like to think that if I had been abducted from a police station and then beaten almost to death, I would also still be able to stay in Zimbabwe. I do not know though if I would. I do not know if I would ever again be able to trust policemen who had watched me being abducted.

Fifteen months after David Stevens was murdered and the five farmers abducted and tortured, I drove to the little town of Murehwa. I did not want to see where the abominations had occurred, I did not want to see blood on the rocks, I just wanted to re-visit the town which was a part of my childhood, reassure myself that normal people lived there and normal things happen there. I wanted to put my own ghosts to rest. Knowing exactly what had gone on there made my visit very traumatic and I am not ashamed to say that I was afraid and nervous and felt extremely uncomfortable as I got closer and closer to the town. Where the main road turns into Murehwa there is a crossroads and as I slowed at the junction I felt a cold chill as I looked across at the dirt road where hell and terror had started for six men.

On the road that leads into Murehwa there is a 60 km speed limit and almost the first complex you come upon is the Murehwa police camp. It all looked so peaceful and normal, so quiet that no one would ever be able to visualise what it had been like 15 months before. Crowds of thugs calling themselves war veterans running down the road, shouting and throwing stones, vehicles streaming in and out, shots being fired, handcuffs and beatings.

I did not have the courage to turn into the Murehwa police camp; I did not want to see the courtyard the farmers had been taken from at gunpoint, I did not even want to see the car park. Glancing down at the speedo in my car I realised that my foot was treading heavily on the accelerator, my body was pushing me away from this place of betrayal and shame. The verge of the road outside the police camp was grazed short by communal cattle; one small bush and an anthill were the only obstructions there and I knew immediately that this was where Gary Luke had taken cover while men with guns shot at John Osborne and Steve Krynauw. Even a bush and an anthill on the side of the road were now places of fear in Murehwa, places that concealed horrors and secrets.

I did not go into the little town; I did not have the courage to drive past the war veterans' headquarters. I had been warned that it was not safe; it was not wise to let my white face be seen in this town. I did not want to see that building either, did not want to visualise six men being beaten, taunted and dragged out of vehicles. Neither did I have the courage to drive through the town and go to the Murehwa caves. The caves are apparently decorated with magnificent rock paintings of prancing antelope, zebra, elephant, buffalo, and five lions. There are paintings too of women, some with babies on their backs and of men with exotic hairstyles. The naked men depicted on the walls of the caves are thought by historians to depict an ancient fertility or initiation rite. As much as I wanted to see these wonderful paintings created by Zimbabwe's first ancestors, I could not go there. How could I look at rock paintings and not hear the cries of anguish, not see the marks left by Stuart Gemmill and Ian Hardy in this place where they were tortured. Their shackled hands and feet must have left marks in the dust, their blood must surely have darkened the soil.

Richie and I set out to climb one big granite kopje that stands behind my mother's home in Murehwa. To him this was an adventure, a great day at his grandmother's house, a grandmother whom I had been too scared to visit for over a year. Even with my continual reminders to him to stay where I could see him, Richie bounded up the smooth granite slope, kicking at stones and sticks, urging me to hurry. 'Come on, Mum, we're nearly there,' he called out over his shoulder, the wind throwing his words back to me as he approached the weather beacon at the top.

'You can do it,' he called, his little face smiling at me almost condescendingly as I picked the most gradual incline to the top. As I walked in the warmth of a glorious spring morning, my arms were covered with goose bumps and I was cold from head to toe. It was quiet all around and yet I could hear so much: shouts, groans, moans, screams. The place was filled with ghosts and angry spirits and I stood with my arm around my son underneath the weather beacon. The workings had long since rusted and even a gale would not have moved the vanes.

As Richie did what all little boys do, threw stones and skimmed them across the rocks, I sat on the warm stone and looked out at the view. It was spectacular, rugged and so African. Granite outcrops and kopjes in every direction, the purple haze of far-off mountains, silvery water trails slithering down smooth grey rocks. You could see for miles from here and as my eyes traversed 360 degrees I saw that at the base of every single hill, kopje and outcrop was a group of houses. There was not one hill that I could see in any direction that did not have homes, people living clustered at its base.

Realisation suddenly dawned. Wherever it was that David Stevens and John Osborne had been taken, someone had seen and heard them. On whichever of these kopjes it was that Steve Krynauw and Gary Luke were beaten, someone had seen and heard them. Stuart Gemmill and Ian Hardy had waited, exposed on the granite until they were rescued somewhere in these hills; they too must have been seen and heard. This whole town not only knew what had happened here but had probably seen and heard parts of that hell too. Some must have been witnesses and others accomplices to murder, torture and brutality. This really was a town with a secret.

Richie was getting bored with my staring and musing and was wandering further and further away. I slipped off my dusty town shoes and walked barefoot on the granite. I wanted to feel the stone underfoot, see how it must have felt for the barefoot farmers who were force-marched up these granite hills. It was both cool and warm, smooth in places and sharp in others. Occasionally it was prickly too as little islands of vegetation sprung up in cracks and depressions in the rock. In places it was slippery – it had been the rainy season when the farmers were here and must have been treacherous. The rock is stained with all manner of lichen, coloured from dull bronze to bright orange and startling green. Rainwater gathers in the hollows and depressions, and it was to these puddles that Ian Hardy and Stuart Gemmill had crawled on their bellies to drink. I stopped and closed my eyes; a warm wind buffeted against me but try as I might I could not shut out the voices. Voices in the wind, shouting, ordering, crying, groaning.

For me the wind, always my friend and comforter, had become my tormentor and persecutor. The wind coursing over the granite kopjes of Murehwa was filled with too many voices and too many secrets. I called Richard and we left.

FOUR

LAUGHTER IN THE WIND

T he horror of the facts behind the murder of David Stevens stayed with me for months. The wounds were reopened when hearings began on the contested parliamentary election results in the High Court in Harare. Despite losing 57 seats in the 2000 elections, President Mugabe continued to reiterate that the opposition would never take power in Zimbabwe. 'I am firmly asserting to you that there will never come a day when the MDC will rule this country – never ever,' he said in Matabeleland North, an area where Zanu PF had lost every single constituency to the opposition in the parliamentary polls. 'Let the Movement for Democratic Change side with the Europeans and the British but we will conquer them together.'

The Never Ever speech was perhaps Mugabe's most damning yet and reminded everyone of a similar pronouncement that had been made by Ian Smith in the dying days of Rhodesia (1976): 'I don't believe in majority rule ever in Rhodesia ... not in a thousand years.' Smith had said that blacks would never rule Zimbabwe, and now President Mugabe was making the same impossible statements.

Perhaps spurred on by the President's speech, war veterans intensified the raids on companies that had been going on for some weeks in Harare and other towns and cities across the country, bringing the terror and violence into everyone's lives.

Speaking in Bulawayo in late February 2001, Chenjerai Hitler Hunzvi ('Hitler' was his chosen middle name) announced openly that war veterans were setting up 'structures' in all urban constituencies to start campaigning for Zanu PF for the 2002 elections. 'We are determined to win back the support which Zanu PF lost in urban areas during the parliamentary elections,' he said. The results of these 'structures' were immediately demonstrated by Joseph Chinotimba, a municipal security guard who rounded up helpers and stormed Trinidad Industries in Msasa on the outskirts of Harare. Barging into a management meeting, Chinotimba ordered the company to stop the retrenchment of 30 workers or face violence.

War veterans also stormed into a management meeting of Dezign Incorporated, another company in Harare's industrial area, and attacked senior executives with iron bars after they refused to reinstate dismissed workers. The company's general and financial managers, both bleeding from head wounds, were then abducted and taken to the Zanu PF headquarters in the centre of the city. After being held for three hours, interrogated and threatened, the men were released when they finally agreed to reinstate the dismissed workers. The company closed down days later, though, and its gates were manned by war veterans who flew a Zimbabwean flag on the roof while millions of dollars were lost in unfilled orders.

Next on Hunzvi and Chinotimba's list was Leno Trading, a public transport company in Harare owned by two Pakistani businessmen. After investing more than Z$200 million in the business, disgruntled workers in a pay dispute called on the assistance of the urban terror brigade. Calling themselves war veterans, the militants seized 22 minibuses and drove them to Zanu PF headquarters and then raided the garage of the businessmen. They assaulted three mechanics, stole diesel and money and proceeded to the home of the men. They scaled the wall, broke into the house and stole a television, video and two vehicles before leaving. Newspapers at first reported that the two Pakistani businessmen had gone into hiding and then that they had both fled the country.

Chinotimba and his gang were unstoppable. They went on to another industrial company in Harare, Resource Drilling. There they 'confiscated' two compressors and a drilling rig, and dumped them at Zanu PF headquarters. It seemed the take-over of equipment was designed to force management to pay hefty retrenchment packages to workers being laid off. Then they went to the Omnia fertiliser company in Harare, abducted a member of the management and demanded Z$20 000 for his release. Money in hand, drunk with power, the urban terrorists went to a cotton company with Chinotimba. There they ordered the immediate reinstatement of 28 retrenched workers, threatening mayhem if their demands were not met.

Buoyed by the continued inaction of the police, no arrests and the continuing silence of companies being attacked, Joseph Chinotimba then proclaimed himself to be the new head of the trade union movement. 'I am now the president of the ZCTU ... The way we solved problems on the farms is the same way we are going to solve industrial issues,' Chinotimba said, clearly seeing himself as a modern day Robin Hood. 'We are now taking over as the labour department of the ruling party to try and deal with these white-owned firms that want to sabotage our economy.'

His words were laughable, but the rhetoric was backed up with visitations, violence and extortion. The Zimbabwe Lawyers for Human Rights issued a statement deploring the illegality and lawlessness, the British Council closed their library and information service and the Canadian High Commissioner to Zimbabwe was assaulted when he tried to intervene as war veterans abducted the director of a Canadian organisation, CARE International. The Harare Children's Home was visited by ex-combatants, the Sanyati Cotton Company offices were taken over, Speciss College, Willowvale Mazda Industries and Cresta were also invaded – and similar reports followed from Gweru, Masvingo and Victoria Falls. Chaos was widespread and all the free newspapers were scathing. 'Where is the President while all hell is breaking loose?' asked the editor in an April *Daily News* leader comment that echoed our thoughts.

As the invasions continued the Minister of Public Service, Labour and Social Welfare, July Moyo, was said to be out of the country and no one in authority was doing anything to stop the chaos. Company invasions spread to other towns and the management of a cotton company in Gokwe were assaulted by war veterans and government supporters who accused them of hiring MDC sympathisers as casual workers for seasonal posts. In Chipinge war veterans invaded the Farm and City Centre, dragged staff members outside and ordered the company to close. The militants accused the management of having fired a security guard who was a war veteran and ordered that he be reinstated. Contacted by newspapers for reports, management refused to comment, saying the matter was 'delicate' – and sadly this fear of speaking out played right into Chinotimba's hands. It reinforced the belief that he and his militants were merely solving labour disputes and fighting for the rights of workers.

President Mugabe then added more fuel to the fire by threatening to take over and nationalise mines and manufacturing companies that were closing down because of the dire state of the economy. Any closures will have to have the assent of government. The welfare of the workers will in every case be the decisive or determining factor. Government will not tolerate any closures. President Mugabe perpetuated the myth that companies were closing down in support of either the MDC or white farmers. With the virtual support of the president, the invasions of businesses continued: other companies to be visited included an engineering firm, a plating company, a brick-making concern, a hospital and a top Harare department store.

The exorbitant amounts of money the war veterans were forcing companies to hand over led to the closure of the Harare's Dental Clinic, which paid out Z$7 million to five former employees. It took a number of weeks for some of the facts behind the company invasions to emerge. One of these was that the militant company raiders demanded a commission from disgruntled ex-employees whom they claimed to represent. These commissions ranged from five to fifteen per cent of the money paid out. The motives of Robin Hood and his Merry Men were certainly not what they had led us to believe.

Hunzvi and Chinotimba went too far with their company invasions, though, when they started on foreign-owned firms. Embassy officials said that eight South African companies in Zimbabwe had been raided and that their staff reported both attacks and abductions at the hands of militants. The International Federation of the Red Cross and Red Crescent Societies moved its seven expatriate families out of Zimbabwe because of concerns for their safety.

Chenjerai Hunzvi then threatened to raid foreign embassies and again put the true political face on the entire issue. 'Our next target after solving workers' problems in factories and companies will be to deal once and for all with foreign embassies and non-governmental organisations who are funding the MDC,' he said. 'We will be visiting them soon to express our displeasure and to warn them to stop interfering with our internal matters. No one can stop us in our second phase.'

In what was to be almost his last public speech, Hunzvi effectively made a nonsense of everything Chinotimba had been claiming. This was nothing to do with righting injustices, it was a blatant case of eliminating political opposition. Hunzvi's words caused an immediate flurry and foreign diplomats met in Harare to assess and review their security and safety. A British Foreign Office spokesman said that they were taking Hunzvi's threats very seriously and were looking for official explanations from the government and assurances about diplomatic protection.

When it seemed as if the entire system was collapsing in front of our eyes, the government suddenly stepped in and made the most ridiculous U-turn. Companies had begun laying workers off and closing down, massive orders were being lost, billions of dollars' worth of revenue was going down the drain. President Mugabe had said nothing, the police had done nothing – and then suddenly Home Affairs Minister John Nkomo stepped in. He could not possibly say what we all knew – that industrial invasions had been designed to intimidate company owners, win over workers and try and win back support for Zanu PF in urban areas – so instead he called a press conference and said that the police would begin arresting company invaders and ordered that they stop immediately.

The new official line being pushed by the state media was that it was not war veterans conducting company invasions but 'impostors'. Joseph Chinotimba, personally involved in a number of the industrial raids, also climbed on the bandwagon and told the press that he himself had given a 'directive' to the police to arrest people guilty of extortion. Now there was no doubt that we were the laughing stock of the world: a municipal security guard was in charge of the country's police force – and they were obeying him too. There was a flurry and much publicity over the arrests of 26 people who were supposed to have been involved in company invasions. They were fall-guys, though, none of the ringleaders was arrested.

For a moment it almost looked as if the entire scam would be exposed when police arrested Mike Moyo, a war veteran and Zanu PF secretary for security in Harare. Moyo spent the weekend in the cells and was incensed. He told the *Zimbabwe Independent* that both Hunzvi and Chinotimba had become instant millionaires through extortion during company invasions and said he would testify to this effect in court. Moyo was clearly not prepared to take the rap for his seniors and spoke out vociferously against Hunzvi. 'Hunzvi has a lot of pending cases. The issue of the Z$13 million meant for war veterans' housing has not been resolved. The ZEXCOM funds disappeared and nothing happened. Hunzvi's term of office as chairman has long expired. He is not a true revolutionary. If you go into history you will see that he was picking mangoes and interacting with whites in Poland when we were in the struggle,' he said. Moyo went further, implicating even the Minister of Home Affairs: 'Nkomo sanctioned these company occupations. The war veterans did not do this alone. I want to sue the Minister for the harassment that I went through in police cells,' he said.

Mike Moyo was released from custody after a weekend in the cells. A court appearance was made but charges were dropped as the state was unable to provide sufficient evidence that he had been involved in company invasions.

After nearly two months of madness the company invasions suddenly stopped as quickly as they had started. Chenjerai Hunzvi disappeared from view amidst growing whispers that he was unwell, and Joseph Chinotimba turned his attention and energies elsewhere. The only sign that for once the government was not as united in its opinions on recent events as it wished us to believe was the sudden resignation of the Minister for International Trade and Development. Nkosana Moyo, in his post for only ten months, left over a weekend, made no public statements at all, shunned all interviews and hastily left the country with his family.

The loss of two Zanu PF ministers through the death of Border Gezi and the departure of Nkosana Moyo in the first few days of May 2001 undoubtedly shook the ruling party. The death of Border Gezi particularly had robbed the party of a prolific campaigner. Throughout the early months of 2000 Gezi had regularly accompanied President Mugabe on his campaign trail. He was young and vibrant and a perfect companion for the septuagenarian president. While Mugabe walked with his characteristic raised and clenched fist, Gezi would attract younger followers by gyrating and dancing the popular 'kwasa-kwasa', much to the delight of the crowds. As Minister of Youth, Sport and Recreation, Gezi made waves wherever he went and whenever he spoke. He set up youth training centres whose graduates would later become men of terror as they campaigned for Zanu PF at all local and national elections. There was nothing small or discreet about Border Gezi, who had a huge beer belly, a large shining face and an enormous flowing beard, and always wore T-shirts with his own picture blazed on the front.

Gezi died when his driver lost control of their vehicle after a tyre burst, and his passing left the government clearly bruised. Zanu PF turned its attention to mayoral elections looming in Masvingo. The province was turned upside down, violence escalated and dozens of people were abducted, beaten and stoned. The Masvingo governor was on record as having told voters in the province that if Zanu PF lost the poll then people would die. The elections were held and when the results were announced they showed the whole country that violence did not always work. Fifty-three-year-old Alois Chaimiti was elected as the new MDC Mayor of Masvingo.

Violence was not confined to the countryside any more: numerous outrages occurred in and around towns and cities, with even MPs from the opposition regularly having their homes stoned and trashed. Condemnation of the increasing violence was widespread and came from the Commonwealth, foreign embassies and diplomatic missions. The Danish embassy announced the suspension until further notice of a Z$100 million a year joint aid programme. The Commonwealth again said how concerned it was about what it called 'the deteriorating situation' in Zimbabwe, but it did nothing, insisting that this was an internal problem, which could only be resolved by Zimbabweans themselves.

The Catholic bishops issued a pastoral letter that was one of the most outspoken statements yet to be made by any of the churches in the country. The Catholics did not mention names but spoke very frankly. 'Violence, intimidation and threats are the tools of failed politicians ... The holders of political power, including those claiming to be Christians, do tend to abuse their fellow human beings ... Public officers come to be associated with self-enrichment and corruption ... The activities of war veterans, in both urban and rural areas, are not solving problems ...'

The US Secretary of State, Colin Powell, was not as lily-livered as his European counterparts. Speaking in Johannesburg, Mr Powell announced that the debts of 19 African countries that had democratic governance were being written off, but Zimbabwe was not one of them. After talks with the South African Foreign Minister on 25 May 2001, Mr Powell said: 'We not only discussed the economic crisis. I concentrated on the political crisis caused to a large extent by the actions of President Mugabe ... Action has to be taken to stabilise the situation and persuade Mr Mugabe to act in a more democratic fashion.'

Zimbabwe's leaders were incensed by Powell's words and Minister of Justice Patrick Chinamasa was on ZBC television that night. 'Powell's words are nonsense. The Americans and British are trying to impose leaders on us.' This statement was one we were to hear thousands of times in the coming months and would later be used as a major election tool by Zanu PF.

Keeping track of everything that was happening in Zimbabwe was like trying to do an enormous jigsaw puzzle with no idea of what the picture was supposed to be. Increasingly I found people both telling me what had happened to them and asking me for information. The bulk of my work was done by e-mail and to try and reduce the load I again started sending out a weekly letter updating the situation and highlighting the horrors and abuses. I had done this regularly in 2000, and then stopped for a few months to concentrate on writing *African Tears*.

When the government-owned telephone company (PTC) disconnected my line I went immediately to their offices in the town. I was shocked to find dozens of people milling angrily around who had also had their telephones disconnected. It was a bit like a who's who in Marondera and included complainants from the main bank, the general hospital, the biggest supermarket, the florist, school headmasters and the chemist. We had all been disconnected, the PTC said, for non-payment of accounts. None of us had received an account, but the PTC said that was not their problem, we were late in paying and would now have to settle our non-existent accounts and pay reconnection fees too. They said that they were unable to generate duplicate accounts and that we should just pay what they said we owed.

One by one we stood in a line, muttering, swearing and complaining – but we paid, what else could we do? I spotted a friendly technician and asked him what was going on. He said the PTC did not have enough money to pay its month-end wage bill – hence the mass disconnections. This was management by crisis: it started at the top of our government and rippled down into every sector of our lives – and we put up with it because there was no option. There was no competition, nowhere to go for better service, and absolutely no point in complaining as it was only met with inaction and anger.

Unrest in Zimbabwe was escalating every day and dissatisfaction was growing in almost every sector of the country. Teachers began to speak out about abuses of their rights, saying they were being forced to pay 'protection money' to war veterans and that demands for money were accompanied by threats of violence. Asked for comment, a regional director for education said: 'It is my first time of hearing this.' This ridiculous statement was one frequently used by a growing number of government officials who attempted to make us believe that even though there were widespread reports, written records and even affidavits of violations and irregularities, they knew nothing about it. It was a statement made hundreds of times by police and even government ministers – and this insult to the intelligence was met by tongue-clicking and resigned shaking of the head by ordinary people.

Since I had spoken out so loudly and for so long, having seen the activities of war veterans at first hand, people seemed to know exactly where I stood and when they wrote, phoned or came to see me they knew they could trust me. I had a visit from a well-known and respected head teacher in my home town that left me deeply saddened. Arriving unexpectedly, Joe (whose name I have changed) looked around him nervously and drove rapidly through the gates. He looked exhausted and worried; his forehead was beaded with sweat, and after we had got through the niceties and with tea at hand he told me what had happened.

A civic group in the town had asked Joe if they could hire the school hall for a public meeting. He had told them that the hall was fully booked and they had left. Two days later Joe was visited, first by the CIO (Central Intelligence Operation), then by the police and finally by the war veterans. Joe was accused by all three groups of supporting the opposition and getting involved in politics. He told them all exactly what had been requested and that he had declined, but his explanations were not acceptable. War veterans came to the school in the afternoon and went from room to room searching classrooms and offices. They looked in desks and cupboards, filing cabinets and drawers searching for anything linking Joe to either the MDC or the civic rights group. When they found nothing, Joe said the war veterans left but came back that night, shouting, taunting and throwing stones on the roof of his house.

Joe told me that this had gone on for two nights; his wife and children were terrified and the whole family was exhausted and stressed to breaking point. 'Anyway' he said, looking over his shoulder for about the hundredth time, 'I came to see you to tell you that now I know exactly how you felt on the farm.'

Joe had been out to the farm a few times in the last weeks before I left and on one occasion had arrived in the middle of a dire crisis when the war veterans had set fire to three different parts of the farm. Now it was his turn.

'It is awful, Joe,' I responded. 'Have they gone now?'

'For now they have gone, but last night I waited and waited for them, for the noise. But they never came.'

'You must try and get some sleep, Joe.'

'Yes, yes,' he said almost impatiently. 'But I had to come and tell you that now I know what it felt like for you. To tell you that no one is safe anymore, no one.'

I sat quietly and looked at this man, in his sixties, exhausted, frightened and very stressed. There was nothing I could say except how lucky it was that it was school holidays and that there had been no children around.

After a couple of minutes Joe composed himself and a slight twinkle came into his eyes. 'They have told me that I must not associate with whites any more!' he said, laughing and shaking his head at the absurdity of it.

'Why, Joe?'

'Aaah,' he sighed, still chuckling. 'They told me that I was a sell-out for having white friends and warned me to stop all communications with white people.'

'So what are you doing here, then, Joe?' I asked, smiling.

'They cannot stop that,' he answered vehemently. 'They cannot stop it.'

We talked for a while longer before Joe left amidst much laughter after we had made up a story he could use as to why he had been visiting me. These were the times we lived in and although we laughed, Joe and I were both enormously saddened that things had come to this. Perhaps things were not like this in the cities, but in a small town like ours nothing was secret; gossip, rumour and speculation were rife.

Another unexpected visitor arrived at my gate shortly after this, with much hugging and hand-slapping, laughter and damp eyes. I hadn't seen Jane for six months – since leaving the farm – and we had a lot of catching up to do. I could not help myself and reached out to touch the ugly, raised scar left by a rod of burning steel that had been pressed into her upper lip. All these months later I still blamed myself for Jane's ordeal at the hands of war veterans on our farm, sure that it wouldn't have happened if I had been there. That was something I would have to come to terms with in the times ahead – for now it was just pure pleasure to hear her laughter and see her wide smile.

After we had caught up on each others' news I went and got a copy of *African Tears* to give to Jane and inside I wrote: 'This is our story, we were together.'

'It is you,' Jane kept repeating as she stroked the front cover again and again.

'It's us, Jane,' I answered. 'It is all of us, our story.'

When it was time for Jane to leave she asked me for a bag to put the book in. She did not want to be seen with it and I felt overwhelmed with sadness, as I had with my other visitor. So very sad that we had to hide our own story, that friendships had to be hidden and meetings had to go on behind closed doors. What had our government done to us?

Independence Day arrived on 18 April 2001 and the country again held its breath waiting to hear from our President. We so rarely saw or heard President Mugabe except on these public occasions and everyone was glued to their television and radio sets. I sat with my notebook on my lap. The President was due to speak at 10.30 am and there was live coverage from 10.00 am. A group of policeman ran around the field of the National Sports Stadium carrying a burning torch, there was confusion for a moment and the ZBC (Zimbabwe Broadcasting Corporation) commentator said: 'It appears that the torch has been dropped.' For the next ten minutes nothing spectacular happened, then the camera focused on a stretcher being carried in. One of the soldiers had fainted, and that caused a stir in the stands of increasingly restless people.

For the next 50 minutes nothing happened and the commentators kept up an incessant dialogue tracking the history of Zimbabwe and particularly praising the land redistribution. Then at 11.00 am the screen went blank. I checked the radio too, and there was an ominous hissing until at last someone broke the static and said there had been a break in power to the stadium. (The following day this break in electricity was blamed on the MDC, who were accused of having sabotaged the cables.) At 11.20 the live coverage returned but still no President appeared. There were dog displays, police displays, music and drum majorettes and finally at 12.30, two hours later than advertised, President Mugabe arrived.

His speech seemed at first frankly realistic. He spoke about a country 'experiencing serious difficulty', about unemployment, inflation, interest rates and floods, but did not offer explanations as to why Zimbabwe was in such a diabolical state. He said that the 'fight against colonialism' had steeled us for 'what we are grappling with today'. He said we were a 'nation in the middle of an historic socio-economic programme' and were correcting an 'inequitable imbalance'.

Then the President voiced his opinions on Britain, and his words were scathing and extremely blunt. Britain's criticism of Zimbabwe's violent and illegal farm seizures, human rights abuses and attacks on the opposition was 'an affront to our sovereignty,' he said. 'We say to Britain here and now: hands off, hands off, don't keep interfering, hands off.' President Mugabe made it very clear that he was not going to change his policies or take any notice of the increasing world criticism.

As a birthday present to the people of Zimbabwe, the government listed 137 more farms they were going to seize and there were the usual question marks as to the reasoning behind the properties listed. Properties to be taken included those belonging to Philip Mpofu, Enock Ntuta, Edward Songo and Charles Sibanda – land was being taken from black Zimbabweans to give to other black Zimbabweans, it made no sense at all on the surface. To those who cared to question the farm listings the reasons were obvious. Anyone who did not support Zanu PF would lose their land, regardless of their colour.

Also listed were ranches, safari farms and the country's only trout farm – but the one causing the biggest uproar was the farm belonging to the Olds family. This family had had two of its members murdered, and now its property gazetted for seizure as well: the only word that came to mind was 'obscene'.

Throughout April and May the listings of farms the government intended to seize continued. To the outsider it was very confusing: the question constantly asked was – did whites really own this many farms? They did not, and the explanation was simple. The moment a farm was delisted, for whatever reason, the government would then gazette it again, and when you took the time to study the lists, the same farms appeared again and again. Some new properties appeared on the lists, but the whole thing was a mess in any case: war veterans and their supporters took over farms regardless of whether they were gazetted for acquisition or not.

Front-page news in the *Zimbabwe Independent* told of how one of the country's most important national parks had been cut up into plots for resettlement. Gonarezhou National Park was part of a massive transfrontier reserve encompassing three countries and was set to be an enormous regional conservation project involving Zimbabwe, Mozambique and South Africa. Two months after the signing of the Transfrontier Agreement, war veterans were resident in Gonarezhou, chopping down trees, removing fences and poaching animals.

The Provincial Governor confirmed that squatters had moved into Gonarezhou, but said that humans and animals would be living side by side and that he did not see this as being a problem. Governor Hungwe clearly did not understand that foreign tourists would hardly come to Zimbabwe to see people and cattle in a wilderness conservation area.

In almost all areas there was mounting evidence that people newly resettled on commercial farms were struggling to survive, let alone grow surplus food. Some spoke to the newspapers and said they simply did not have the resources to farm the land they had been allocated. In Masvingo one new settler said to the *Daily News*: 'It's like waiting for a bus that will never come. We were made to believe that everything was going to be provided for us as soon as we got to the farms. Now we are as good as people who have been dumped in a jungle without food and left to die at the mercy of marauding wolves. This land issue is a political gimmick.'

In the Midlands the Provincial Governor admitted that 700 000 people had applied for food aid in the area and described the situation in some districts as being 'desperate'. In both Manicaland and Matabeleland, government officials admitted that the land redistribution exercise had not benefited the right people and that mostly it was policemen, CIO officers, municipal workers and civil servants who had been given plots on acquired farms.

One small scandal that went almost unnoticed was the sudden eviction of 200 settlers from a farm in Mvuma. Riot police and Zanu PF officials moved into Gadzanga Farm in the middle of the night. They burnt down huts and loaded squatters into trucks, dumping them on the road outside Mvuma police station. The farm, part of Central Estates, belonged to a white man, Nick van Hoogstraten, an absentee landlord, British business tycoon and long-time financial backer of Zanu PF.

Analysts began talking about reduced wheat harvests and economists warned of shortages of up to 800 000 metric tonnes. Towards the end of May 2001 the government announced that all wheat exports had been suspended until further notice – but the agriculture minister still insisted that there was not going to be a shortage of food. Dr Made said he had frozen trade in wheat to make sure that the country would not have to import the grain.

One of the worst reports came in the *Financial Gazette* under the headline: 'War vets steal $1 million aid for cyclone victims.' The European Union had donated money to feed people displaced by flooding, and the German aid group, Help, was tasked with distribution to people in need. War veterans in Chimanimani, however, decided that they were better qualified to identify people in need and they broke into an asbestos warehouse and simply took everything – maize, sugar beans, salt and cooking oil.

The EU delegation head sent an immediate protest to the Zimbabwe government. Neither Foreign Minister Stan Mudenge nor Permanent Secretary Willard Chiwewe was available for comment, but police confirmed the incident and made the standard statement that 'investigations are in progress.' Anywhere else in the world the Agriculture Minister would have been forced to resign immediately from his post for having allowed such a situation, but not in Zimbabwe. Dr Made was in President Mugabe's pocket and was clearly going to keep up the pretence that everything was rosy.

The growing shortage of food was already beginning to take its toll and it was the youngest and most vulnerable in Zimbabwe who were the worst affected. Dr Chris Tapfumaneyi, the medical superintendent of Harare Central Hospital, reported that child malnutrition was on the increase and that over eighty per cent of the children in the paediatric unit were underfed. Over a thousand children had been admitted to the hospital in January 2001 suffering from malnutrition, a figure almost double that of the previous year. Dr Tapfumaneyi went on to report that the situation was being exacerbated by the chronic shortage of drugs in the country and said that nine children were dying at the hospital every week. The doctor told reporters that at his hospital there were no anaesthetics or post-operative drugs and there was a chronic shortage of antibiotics.

The situation was no better at Harare's Parirenyatwa Hospital, whose drug-making department had been forced to close. A doctor there said that drugs at the hospital were in chronically short supply because the department was operating with five pharmacists instead of 14 and six technicians instead of ten. The Minister of Health, Dr Timothy Stamps, admitted there was a serious shortage of drugs and staff, but did not explain why nurses in some areas were being dismissed by war veterans who accused them of being MDC supporters.

Illegally dismissed nurses were being replaced by army personnel – which may have explained an e-mail doing the rounds which contained comments apparently taken from patients' cards at Parirenyatwa Hospital. There were some classics:

'Patient has chest pain if she lies on her left side for over a year.

'On the second day the knee was better and on the third it disappeared.

'Discharge status: Alive but without my permission.

'The patient refused autopsy.

'Patient has left white blood cells at another hospital.

'Patient had waffles for breakfast and anorexia for lunch.
'She is numb from her toes down.
'Rectal examination revealed a normal sized thyroid.
'Both breasts are equal and reactive to light and accommodation.
'Examination of genitalia reveals that he is circus sized.
'Skin: somewhat pale but present.
'The pelvic exam will be done later on the floor.'

Health had become the topic on everyone's lips in the winter of 2001 and there were gossip, rumour and speculation about the health of war veteran leader Chenjerai Hunzvi. The ZBC made infrequent reports, saying sometimes that Hunzvi had influenza, then malaria. When he collapsed in Bulawayo there were rumours that he was in a coma; no journalists were allowed to see him and two who tried had the film ripped out of their cameras. The government and other war veterans emphatically and repeatedly announced that Hunzvi was neither critically ill nor dead, but simply recovering from a particularly nasty bout of malaria and wished his privacy to be respected.

By the end of May I could not find any more excuses to stop me from going back to Stow Farm. It was a visit I had been putting off for months, because I really did not want to remember what my life had been like. I did not want to see what had become of the place I had called home for a decade. I wanted to remember the good things from my life there and not see any of the things that would remind me of the year from hell when war veterans had taken over my life. But I had to go back and face my ghosts.

I drove out alone along the familiar road on a clear winter morning. It was a road I knew well, every bump and rock, every pothole and hump, but still I drove slowly, perhaps delaying the inevitable. Everything was very familiar and yet so strange. The closer I got to the farm, the faster I found myself driving, but it did not stop me from seeing things through the boundary fence that I did not want to see. The scraggly, collapsing huts, built by the war veterans and their helpers using our poles and on our land, were still littered in the fields. The fences were gone in some places, collapsed in others and repaired in a few. The plantations of gum trees that once stood in proud, dense blocks were thin and ugly, still showing the scars of the massive harvesting undertaken by the war veterans. There was only one field obviously being used, and here less than two dozen dairy cows grazed in the browning winter grass. I knew it was stupid, but I couldn't stop myself from remembering how these fields had looked. Charolais cows, Brahman bulls, calves and weaners; ewes, rams and lambs – the fields had been bursting with life, and now there was almost nothing.

There may have been nothing to see physically, but in my mind's eye there was so much, so many memories and adventures had taken place in these now almost barren fields. For the first time I felt ashamed to admit that I was the co-owner of this farm. Once our pride and joy, it was now rambling, weed-infested and broken down. I turned in at the driveway on the main road and the gate was closed and padlocked. Grass grew up thickly along the edges and down the centre of the driveway and the place looked completely deserted. I hooted and shouted but no one came. I turned off the engine and for a couple of minutes sat in silence, staring at the gum trees that stood tall on the inside of the gate. Getting out of my truck, I leant against the door, closed my eyes and listened to the wind in the trees. I had not realised how much I missed the farm, the trees, the solitude and the wind.

Mostly I missed the wind, and for a few minutes I allowed it to penetrate my consciousness. It was as if I could hear the memories of the past in the wind whispering through the leaves of the towering gum trees I had planted with my own hands. I could hear the gentle creaking of the pram as I pushed my newborn baby backwards and forwards to calm him. I could hear the rustling of birds fidgeting in the branches or uttering alarms as they spotted a snake in the grass below. I could hear Richard calling to his friends and see them using the saplings as swings, hanging, laughing and dropping to the ground. I could hear Jane's voice calling to me, at first her laughter-filled greeting and then her terrified urgent shouts for me to run from the war veterans who were coming. The wind was filled with sounds and memories; there was laughter in the wind, but also fear and anger.

My thoughts and memories were interrupted by a man with an enormous bunch of keys who had come to unlock the gate. The young couple who had leased the farm both worked in the nearby town, and they ran only a few dairy cows which were left in the care of three workers throughout the week. The man let me in and the tears were heavy and hot on my face as I drove down the driveway towards the storeroom. Everything looked so shabby and uncared for. Everywhere the grass was tall and filled with weeds and blackjacks. Grass runners climbed into the security fence and wound around young trees and shrubs once lovingly tended. The black shade cloth that had covered my greenhouse was tattered and torn and shredding in the wind.

I looked through into what had been my oasis of quiet and beauty in the remnants of the shade house. The few plants I had left behind were dead, their pots crowded with weeds and grass. My lavender bush, still flowering prolifically as it had always done, was tall and scraggly, wound through with grass and its trunk black with powdery mildew. The one hanging basket I had left behind was still alive. Known as Christ on the Cross, the orchid had none of its glorious crimson flowers now and its airborne roots hung down over a metre searching for water, and for love.

Nearby the chicken house, which had always been filled with gossiping layers, was empty, silent and desolate. Through the security fence I looked across to the house, but did not want to see too much. The lawn was unmown, flowerbeds undefined and grown over with weeds and grass. At the nearby tobacco barns someone had smashed out all the grates and doors of the fireboxes and the ground was littered with chunks of rubble. What had been the lush night paddocks where I had weaned and fattened lambs were completely gone. All the kikuyu grass had been dug out and replaced with vegetables; rape and cabbages grew prolifically on the manure-laden soil.

I knew how hard it was, how much back-breaking work it took to keep the farm well tended, and did not blame the tenants who were only here at night and were, like us all, desperately trying to survive and make ends meet. I collected the few things I had come for and left the farm. There were too many memories and I knew I would not want to come back again in a hurry. There was still so much laughter in the wind, and so many tears too.

FIVE

OCEANS OF PEACE

lmost half-way into 2001 the situation in Zimbabwe was beyond belief. There were daily reports of ordinary people suffering the most barbaric outrages at the hands of government supporters. Rape was just one of the horrors – and few were willing to talk about what had happened to them. This is just one story of gang rape that took place shortly after the political madness began in Zimbabwe in 2000. Names have been changed to protect identities.

'You are now our enemies because you really have behaved as enemies of Zimbabwe. We are full of anger.' Those were the words spoken by President Robert Mugabe on Zimbabwe's 20th Independence Day. It was 18 April 2000 and the enemies that the President referred to were white Zimbabweans.

That night two white Zimbabwean women, 'enemies of the state,' were gang raped in a cottage on a farm near Harare airport and a man was brutally assaulted and forced to watch his wife being abused. The three people were not farmers; they just happened to live in a cottage on a farm. They were all innocent victims who got caught up in the backwash of the tide of hate that Mugabe's rhetoric always unleashed.

James and his wife Dawn were having supper when the telephone rang. Dawn's 17-year-old sister, Helen, was with them and the two women sat quietly listening as James talked to his brother on the telephone. They were in Dawn's small dining room with the newly painted ochre walls that matched the red tiles on the floor and reminded Dawn of the colours of an African sunset.

Dawn loved the little cottage she and James rented. They had only been there for three months but she had made it into a cosy and comfortable home. It was a typical farm cottage with small dark rooms and even smaller windows, but Dawn had painted most of it white and hung bright curtains to attract the light. Dawn had made all the curtains herself, mixing colours in some rooms to make what she called her little patchwork cottage. She had painted the lounge burnt orange and decorated the walls with paintings of bright yellow sunflowers. The cottage had three small bedrooms, one of which Dawn and James had converted into a study. The windows in this room were bigger and hung with orange and white net curtains that caught the light and allowed the sun to stream into the room. In the study they had set up their computer and it was a quiet and peaceful room to work in. The bedrooms were fitted with blue wall-to-wall carpets and throughout the rest of the cottage Dawn had scattered brown and cream rugs on the concrete floors.

James came back to the dining room and sat at the solid, dark table, which had belonged to his grandfather. He told Dawn and Helen why his brother had phoned: President Mugabe had been interviewed that afternoon on television. 'Whites are enemies of the State,' the President had said, 'and the country is full of anger.'

James, Dawn and Helen talked quietly for a few minutes. Perhaps it would be safer for them to go into Harare for the night; perhaps it was dangerous to stay in their cottage on a farm just outside Harare. Although their cottage was only eight kilometres from the international airport, it was lonely and isolated. Their nearest neighbours were the owners of the farm, but their house was not even visible from the cottage. In between there were paddocks where sheep and cattle grazed, fields where yellow, red and orange flowers were grown for export, and a big timber plant-ation.

James and Dawn discussed their options but the cottage was their home and neither was keen to leave. The words of President Mugabe were frightening, but, they reasoned, surely that's all they were, just words, simple rhetoric. The three sat talking a while longer. Their conversation was on the usual topic – what was happening in Zimbabwe, why the police were not doing their jobs, why the President had suddenly declared war on whites. The three knew that this was all to do with the war veterans who had moved onto farms with the blessing of the government. They knew that the words of racial hatred came from an angry and bitter President who had been defeated in a constitutional referendum. James, Dawn and Helen did not take the President's words lightly, though. In the last week two white farmers had been murdered and five others had been abducted and tortured. None of them knew what effect the President's words would have on the war veterans squatting on farms. When there was nothing more to say – and because there were no answers – the two women got up from the table. Helen went to the little study and switched on the computer. Dawn stepped outside onto the small front veranda to retrieve the tea tray.

The veranda looked onto a large open garden with views of the farm beyond, but it was dark and Dawn could see nothing as she bent and lifted the tray off the wicker table. Suddenly she heard the sound of running feet, lots of them. With the lights on in the cottage behind her, Dawn struggled to see into the darkness of the garden. Her eyes did not have time to focus, she did not even get a chance to call out to James. Six men swarmed onto the veranda and one made straight for Dawn. The tea tray clattered out of Dawn's hands. Cups, sugar, milk and teapot crashed around her feet and she screamed shortly, twice, before her voice was silenced as a pair of hands closed around her throat. The man shouted instructions to the other men in Shona and he glared at Dawn and hissed: 'Make noise and I kill you. I kill you.' Dawn did not make another sound; she could barely breathe with the man's hands around her throat and did not know where all the other men had gone. She could not warn her husband or sister that a mob of men had gone into the house.

James was walking from the dining room to the kitchen when he heard his wife's scream. He turned immediately towards the veranda but it was already too late. Four men were coming at him, one with a brick in his hand, another with a knife. As the men grabbed James he shouted: 'Leave us, please, leave the people in the house.' James' pleas for mercy were ignored and he was helpless as they grabbed him by the arms. Again James called out, this time in Shona, a language he knew his attackers would understand. *'Siya, siya.'* (Leave us, leave us.)

James's calls went unnoticed and he struggled desperately. His attackers were talking in Shona and he understood what they were saying: 'This is the one we must be careful of. Get him quick.' One of the men slammed a brick into his face, breaking his nose, but still he fought them, struggling but helpless and overpowered. James was dragged into the kitchen, beaten and kicked before being jerked to his knees by his testicles. His ankles and wrists were bound tightly with electric cable. 'Make noise and we kill you,' the men hissed. The knife he had seen earlier sliced through James's hand, but the pain was fuddled and dulled as he drifted in and out of consciousness. He was dumped on the kitchen floor, sure that he was going to be killed, unable to help himself, his wife or his sister-in-law.

Walking backwards, Dawn's attacker dragged her by the throat into the cottage, saying over and over: 'I kill you, I kill you.' Dawn was dropped on the floor in the kitchen and the first thing she saw as the oxygen flooded back into her body was her husband. James was kneeling on the floor, his head on the ground, his wrists bound behind his back. The floor was awash with blood; it was everywhere, making little rivers as it ran between the ceramic tiles. James was dead, she was sure of it.

One of the men slipped in the blood and Dawn suddenly felt all the fear and adrenalin leave her, thinking she would soon be dead too. She had no clear thoughts, no panic or fear, no sadness or terror, just an overwhelming sense of desolation.

The men were all around and began spitting questions at her: 'Where is the gun? Where is the money?'

Dawn didn't tell them; she thought she was going to die anyway.

Men surrounded Dawn and held her down as they tied up her wrists and ankles. The wrist ties were so tight that they were stopping the blood from reaching her fingers, which began to feel numb. Someone snatched a tea towel off a hook by the sink and bound it around her mouth.

Dawn was pushed into a lying position on the kitchen floor. Someone grabbed her feet and dragged her out of the room. She was dragged over the smooth cement floors and for a moment she focused on the immediate reality of the event. There were small rugs on the cement floor and they balled up under her thighs and back as the man pulled her. There were two small steps in the passageway and her head cracked into the cement floor as she was pulled over them. She was dragged into the master bedroom, her own bedroom, and dumped, half-sitting, half-lying against the wall. The men had already been here. Everything had been pulled out of the cupboards – shoes, clothes and papers – and was strewn all over the floor.

One of the men picked up a bottle-green silk shirt and tied it over Dawn's head, securing it around her throat. She could not see any more but she heard the lights being clicked on and off. On and off. On and off. Dawn focused on the sound; it crashed loudly in her head, but soon it was impossible to tell if the lights were on or off. She couldn't see through the shirt, but the light silk flapped against her face as she breathed in and out. In and out. In and out. Breathing. It was all she could concentrate on, that and the tickling, sucking of the silk against her nose.

For a while Dawn seemed to have been left alone and when breathing became less of an effort she began to become more aware of the noises coming from the rest of the cottage. She could hear sobbing noises, loud and guttural, and words that were more noises and grunts than words. She did not know that the noises she could hear were coming from her sister Helen, the sounds she made as she desperately tried to suck air into her lungs. The guttural noises were Helen trying to answer the questions being asked by her attackers: 'Who are you going to vote for?' they were demanding.

Helen was trying to answer them, trying to tell them she was too young to vote, trying to tell them she was just out of school, just a child, but she couldn't make the words sound like words as she fought for breath. She was still in the study. When Dawn had screamed, she had looked out and seen men swarming into the house. She had hidden in the cupboard with a golf club as her only protection against half a dozen crazed men. For 45 minutes Helen had stayed hidden, but when the attackers had started searching the house for valuables, opening cupboards and drawers, there was nowhere to hide and she had been discovered.

Dawn listened and tried to make sense of the things she could hear. There were noises coming from all over the cottage. Someone was shouting what sounded like orders and instructions; the contents of the house were being gathered up. There was obviously someone in charge, directing everything. They must have found the airgun James used to shoot birds, as Dawn had felt the muzzle of it pressed against her head. The safe in the bathroom had also been discovered because she heard loud banging as the men used something large and heavy to break it open.

The cuckoo clock announced the time. Eight-thirty. They had been there for one hour. Dawn heard something heavy being dragged down the passage and deposited next to her. When she heard breathing she knew that it was her husband, but didn't feel any relief at him still being alive, convinced they would both be dead within a few hours. Each time one of the men came into the room or anywhere near the couple, Dawn prepared to die. She was not afraid, she just wanted it to be all over.

From James's breathing Dawn could tell that he was conscious, and she whispered his name. 'James!' He didn't respond at first, afraid perhaps that someone would hear. 'James,' she whispered again. When he answered quietly, Dawn told him that she loved him and he told her he loved her. Dawn did not want to die without James knowing that she loved him, utterly.

Someone heard them whispering and shouted: 'No talking, we kill you. We kill you!' Dawn nodded to indicate that she understood. She knew she had been foolish, but it was incredibly important to her that James knew she loved him.

Dawn heard someone approaching and felt her shorts being slit with a knife. She knew what was coming and struggled, but the knife was pressed against her thigh.

'I cut you!' he said.

Dawn stopped struggling.

The man pushed his knees between her thighs and kept saying 'open', which was impossible because her ankles were strapped together. The man realised this, slashed the ties with the knife and forced her legs apart.

The man raped Dawn and later another man raped her again. There was nothing she could do: she simply lay on her bedroom carpet waiting for whatever they were going to do next. She knew James was still there, listening to it, unable to stop his wife from being raped.

Dawn lay, half naked, for what seemed like about ten minutes, and then, surprisingly, someone covered her with what felt like a towel.

The cuckoo called again; another half hour had passed, and things began to get more frightening. Dawn could smell the distinct, choking smell of petrol; it sounded like they were pouring it all over the house. The slopping, glugging sound of the liquid was terrifying:

she realised they were going to be burned alive; these men were going to burn the cottage down. Then she heard James being pulled out of the bedroom.

Dawn was completely alone and cold terror took over. Suddenly she didn't want to die; she wanted to live. She began to struggle desperately. One of the thongs used to tie her wrists was elastic and she managed to wriggle her thumb out. Once her thumb was free the battle was won and Dawn stripped her hands out of their shackles. She immediately lifted the shirt from her head, pulled off the cloth bound round her mouth and saw that the bedroom door was shut. The curtains were closed and the lights were on and she saw the reddish liquid, the petrol, staining and soaking into the carpet.

Hearing a noise, Dawn quickly put the shirt back over her face, hands behind her back and lay down again. When nothing happened she realised that the noise, the bang, must have been the men leaving. She quickly got up, opened the door and looked into the passageway. She had to try and find her husband and sister quickly, not knowing how long she had before the petrol that had been splashed everywhere would be ignited.

It didn't take long for Dawn to find her husband. James was lying on the floor in the next room. He was still, so still that Dawn feared the worst. She called his name and tried to rouse him and when he didn't respond she ran across to the study to at least try and save her sister. Helen was on the study floor, tied up and with a towel over her body. She was half sitting up, obviously in a bid to escape, and her face filled with horror at the sight of the door opening.

The moment Helen saw her sister, her face flooded with relief. 'They raped me,' she sobbed. 'It's all right ... they raped me too. It's all right now, we're going to be fine,' Dawn said, embracing her sister. She untied Helen's wrists and quickly told her sister that the whole cottage had been doused in petrol and they had no time to waste. Leaving Helen to try and revive James, Dawn tried to phone for help. She thought they would need an ambulance for James because he would be far too heavy for them to carry.

Dawn raced around the house, locking and bolting all the doors so that the men couldn't come back in without her knowledge. She searched the house for a cell phone, or keys for the car. All were gone, four mobile phones, and the wires to the land line were cut too. She saw that a log had been dragged out of the fireplace, clearly in an attempt to ignite the petrol, but it had not worked – and that at least put the fear of a fire into the background. She went back to the little bedroom where James was.

A flood of emotions engulfed Dawn when she saw that James had recovered consciousness. Her pale blue eyes brimmed with tears as she looked at this man whom she loved so much. She had to suppress both her tears and the overwhelming relief, though, and take charge. There was only one thing to do – walk to Harare International Airport, eight kilometres away. It was going to take every ounce of strength and stamina the three had left, but Dawn was convinced that the safest thing was to get out of that house, as fast as they could. She had no way of knowing what was going on on surrounding farms, but she was not going to take any chances.

The three spent a few minutes comforting and reassuring one another, getting their strength back and deciding on the route they should take away from this house of horror. All the clothes in the cottage had been looted by the six men; Dawn had nothing to wear except the shorts that had been cut and were in tatters like a short raggedy skirt, one side longer than the other. Helen managed to find some jeans, and they picked up their passports, which, strangely, had been left lying on the floor. They put their documents and a few coins they found on the floor into a plastic bag and held onto it: at that moment all their worldly possessions were in that one cheap little bag.

James was still wearing his shoes, so would cope with the five-mile walk, and Helen found a pair of boots which, although too small, would have to do. All Dawn could find to put on her feet were a fancy pair of high-heeled shoes made for a friend's wedding. Before they left they and had one last look around the remains of their lives. All of Dawn's jewellery had been stolen, except for the engagement and wedding rings on her finger, but James found an abandoned golf club. It was the only thing he could use to protect Dawn and Helen, and he picked it up as they left the little cottage.

They had agreed to stay away from the main gate in the fence surrounding the garden, as they had no idea where their attackers were. That left them with an eight-foot fence topped with barbed wire to climb and all three were cut and scratched as they struggled their way over. For Dawn, those cuts from the barbed wire fence were to be the only physical reminders of that night when the President of Zimbabwe declared white people to be 'enemies of the state'.

James, Dawn and Helen started to walk across the field, making their way towards the dense bush on the other side, when they heard running. In the moonlight were 50 white Brahman cattle looking like a ghostly nightmare. Particularly for Dawn, the sound of running was terrifying. The running of cattle in a field instantly became the running of men storming her home, grabbing her by the throat. The cattle were just being curious, though, and James quickly guided his wife and sister-in-law through and beyond the animals and towards their destination. James walked in front; Dawn and Helen, holding hands and comforting each other, trailed behind as they struggled through the bush, across a small stream and then underneath the strands of an electric fence as they neared the airport terminal. The five-mile walk took them over an hour. They stopped often to hug and reassure one another, and they vowed not to let the horrors of this night destroy them.

Soon there were no more fields they could go through, and the three were forced to walk on the tarmac as they approached the airport. They trusted no one, had no idea of where or who their attackers were, and every time a vehicle approached they hid in the long grass edging the road. When they came into the light outside the airport buildings there could have been no mistaking the fact that they had been through hell. James was cut on his hands and face and was covered in blood, Dawn was wearing the hacked, raggedy shorts, and all three were covered in scratches and grazes.

Depositing the golf club in a flowerbed outside the terminal, James and the two women walked into the glare of lights at the airport concourse. All the evening flights had departed and few people were around, but the Air Zimbabwe information desk was still open and manned. Dawn breathed an immense sigh of relief: exhaustion began to encroach on her senses and tears were very close as they approached civilisation. She thought that at last the nightmare was over.

Approaching the information desk, they asked to use a telephone. They must have looked as though they needed help, but the woman behind the desk resolutely refused to let them use the phone. James said: 'We need help, we need to get to a hospital.

Please let us use the phone.' The woman behind the desk refused, and they looked around to see if they could borrow a mobile phone, but the few people nearby walked away. The three attracted a lot of very strange looks; strange looks from strangers who did not want to get involved, were not prepared to help.

In view of the political madness that engulfed Zimbabwe and the uncountable examples of police partiality, James, Dawn and Helen did not feel they could report their hell to the police who were at the Harare Airport that evening. They did finally manage to persuade a policeman to let them use a telephone, though, and Dawn immediately called her aunt in the city. As the three waited outside the terminal for Dawn's aunt, a man approached them and told them that it was imperative they make a report to the police and get a report number; he persuaded them to make the attack official.

James had begun to answer a policeman's questions when Dawn's uncle arrived. When it was her turn to speak, the words were not at all easy; speaking them translated the nightmare from hell into instant reality. She struggled to actually say that foul word, 'rape'. It came out softly, barely a whisper, and the policeman did not hear her. Dawn was ashamed, afraid that people would hear. She said it again, louder, telling herself at the same time that she had nothing to be ashamed of but not quite believing her own thoughts.

At last the ordeal was over and the crime reported. James, Helen and Dawn got into the car; safety and security were theirs at last. Dawn's uncle had brought blankets and sweet drinks and he wrapped the two women in the warmth and told them to drink. With security and safety came shock and Dawn started to shake and cry uncontrollably. She was ashamed of her crying, ashamed of her weakness, but it was uncontrollable.

For Dawn, Helen and James, the security of the hospital should have been the end of their ordeal. It had been over four hours since the attack; they were filthy, lacerated, bruised and in deep shock. They should have been met with professional, gentle and compassionate hands, but this was not to be. They were told this hospital did not deal with criminal cases involving he police. So they got back into the car and went to another hospital.

At the next hospital photographs were taken of James before he was treated and had his wounds stitched. Dawn would not leave his side and it was only after her husband had been attended to that the doctors turned to her. They told Dawn and Helen that they did not have any rape kits in the hospital, that they were kept by the police. The doctors had contacted the police to have the kits sent to the hospital. The two women waited and waited. A gynaecologist arrived, asked lots of questions and marked all Dawn's and Helen's injuries on a chart. At about 4.00 am they were told that the police did not have any rape kits either. The gynaecologist said that Dawn and Helen would either have to be admitted to the hospital or go home and return to his office in the morning. Dawn and Helen chose to go home to their uncle's house, but had to promise that they would not wash at all.

Nine hours after being attacked in her own home, having her hands and feet bound, being gagged and blindfolded and raped by two men, Dawn went to her uncle's home. Nine hours after being raped, she was not allowed to wash herself, not allowed to even begin the physical cleansing of her body, because the Zimbabwe police had been unable to provide a rape kit.

The following morning Dawn and Helen returned to the offices of the gynaecologist they had seen the night before. When they got there, they were told that he still hadn't been able to locate a rape kit; that there appeared to be none in Harare. But this specialist knew what was entailed and he took swabs and carefully recorded every detail. Dawn felt detached, as if her body belonged to someone else. She felt so emotionally dead that she thought nothing could hurt her any more.

Helen and Dawn were immediately prescribed antibiotics and AZT drugs, the latter in case Aids was a possibility, in case the men who had raped them were infected with the deadly virus. Coping with the psychological trauma of being raped was something that they would have to bear in the months and years ahead; dealing with the virus had to be coped with immediately. The course of drugs had to be started within 48 hours of the rape if they were to be effective in blocking HIV infection, and there was no way of avoiding their side effects. Dawn immediately began to suffer from the side effects and continued to do so as she and her sister, husband and parents all prepared to leave Zimbabwe.

Dawn was determined that the attack and multiple rape were not going to consume her so she went back to the scene of the crime before departure. 'I did go back to the house before we left for good.

I wanted to face my terror, and I did not want to think of it as a place of misery for me. It was terrifying, but good for me too. I realised that monsters didn't live there and that we had happy times there too.'

Staying in Zimbabwe was not an option for Dawn and her family. 'I think I would have found it much more difficult to stay. In a sense I was running away, but also I needed a new start, and I needed more than anything to live somewhere where I could have a normal life and not live in constant fear. I could not have stayed without going mad with always looking over my shoulder.'

Met by a doctor at the airport in Cape Town, Dawn and Helen were given the first of three monthly injections for Hepatitis B, and Dawn's medication was changed to try and reduce the incessant nausea caused by the AZT drugs, nausea and lethargy that lasted for a month. 'The drugs made us very ill. During that entire time I was constantly nauseous; it is the only time I have ever thought of vomiting as a luxury. I had to keep the drugs in my stomach, my life could depend on it.'

During the month that Dawn and her family stayed in Cape Town, they managed to restore some balance and sanity to their lives. Dawn saw a counsellor and began the process of healing – a process that has continued, and seen Dawn transformed into an amazing, thoughtful and inspirational woman. She was determined not to be a victim. 'I have made a conscious choice to accept what was done, accepted responsibility for only what it is mine to accept and no more, and made a decision to deal with it. So many times I would have liked to take the victim's role and curl up in a corner, but gritting my teeth and taking small steps has helped.'

Dawn also drew great comfort from the fact that she had not been alone at the time of the attack and as she began the process of healing, so too did her husband and sister. 'We are lucky in the way that we shared this experience. It didn't just happen to one or the other, we all went through it together, and we have a very strong bond as a result. The fact that we all survived is the most precious gift, and we keep this in mind most of the time. We are our own therapy group!'

A month after the attack, Dawn and her family left Cape Town for England, where they began to pick up the threads of what was to become their new life. It was not an easy adjustment, and there were still a lot of hurdles to meet and overcome. Dawn's memory of the sound of running feet still sometimes takes her back to the night of the attack. 'Our flat is on the first floor of a house and we have a flight of stairs from our front door to the first floor. People always run up the stairs and it makes my heart stop with fear.'

Dawn and her family will always remember 18 April 2000. I made contact with Dawn for the first time one day before the first anniversary of the attack and hoped that I would not be re-opening old wounds, but felt a real need to reach out and to let her know she was not alone, had not been forgotten. Her response a couple of days later gave me enormous hope and encouragement.

'The anniversary of our attack was yesterday. It was a thoughtful, happy day. A day of celebration, for being alive. We are well, so very well, and have everything to be grateful for. We have settled down here in London so well, we have no regrets and this allows us to completely throw ourselves into our very full lives. As I tell my loving friends, 'reminders' of the attack are not a shock and do not open wounds. The scars will evermore be etched, will never go away, a constant aspect. So when someone brings up the subject it cannot remind me, since I have not forgotten. I do not wish to forget because it is now a part of me.'

Dawn's strength was such an eye-opener to me that I put her in touch with a friend who had also been a victim of the terror in Zimbabwe. Her words to him were inspirational. 'These past few days expecting your letter have been very therapeutic and thoughtful ones. Since it has just been the anniversary of the attack, I think now is a good time to step forward once again and take stock of my life. Ever since the attack, I have found inside me more compassion for others in similar situations than I have ever felt before. And reading your brief description of your attack made my heart beat faster, the adrenalin pulse, and the images appeared. I have a measure of what you went through and you probably felt the same when you read of our experience. I know exactly what you mean about people comparing experiences; they are all bad, and they cannot compare. Each one is unique and each is the worst thing we have ever lived through.'

Dawn was clearly well on the way to healing – and like so many thousands of Zimbabweans, she had come face to face with death. The experience had left her with thoughts familiar to many of us. 'I have learned the value of life. I nearly lost it. I would never again talk so easily of dying, but at the same time I am no longer afraid of it. It was so near and I wasn't afraid. I have no doubt that we were supposed to have been killed, and no doubt that we are alive by a miracle. The thought of dying isn't as frightening as trying to survive it, to live. When I realised what was happening I was very afraid but when I realised that I was going to die, I wasn't afraid. And then when I realised we might live, I was afraid again.'

Dawn's words made complete sense to me and to others who had encountered a closeness to their own mortality. She had been strangled, threatened, tied up, raped and then felt and smelt petrol being poured on and around her. Her need to talk about the experience was as great as mine had been. 'I try to encourage all our friends and family to discuss it with us at any time they want to, but there is a sense of them not wanting to disturb us. I feel sometimes like we're being tiptoed around, as if they feel one wrong word may set off an explosion. Our excellent counsellor in Cape Town gave some very helpful advice with regard to this. She said that we should be understanding with others' not understanding. I have had to remember her words often.'

The weeks and months of recovery have not always been plain sailing for Dawn. 'I must admit that writing about how we are now is relatively easy in comparison with reliving the memories of what actually happened. A small detail came back to me today as I was thinking about it, and it made me feel humiliated and ashamed. I know that these feelings are normal and should be dealt with with a firm hand, and should be worked through in order for them not to make me feel this way any more. It takes strength and it takes determination, and I have that in droves.'

Dawn's strength and determination have helped her decide to write a book about her attack and rape on Zimbabwe's 20th anniversary of independence. 'I will be writing not so much the story of Zimbabwe, but more of my and James's story and how we have coped with it. I intend it to be a book of encouragement and a bit of a self-help book too … If I can help show that people can survive these experiences well and come out on the good side, or if the reason it happened to us was to save it happening to someone else, then these are all good reasons … Tears roll and emotions are high, but it is cleansing. This and the determination that if I don't overcome this, then they have won, and I just will not allow that to happen. I have simply taken each day and each moment one at a time.'

Thoughts of vengeance are not a part of the healing process for Dawn, nor for many of the other Zimbabweans who have been the victims of almost two years of terror attacks. 'The criminals who attacked us will probably never be bought to justice. The police reports and medical reports have all mysteriously disappeared. I have accepted this state of affairs, and don't expect anything to be done about it. In a way it has helped me to recover without it, and I am not waiting for revenge or anything like that. It has been hard, I must admit, and sometimes I wish all kinds of hell on them, but I am a firm believer in what goes around comes around, and they will get their comeuppance. I have some peace with regard to this.'

For the most part, revenge and anger are counterproductive to all of us who have been made victims by men masquerading as 'war veterans' in Zimbabwe's dirty political war. Thousands of crimes have been pushed under the carpet in Zimbabwe over the last two years. Many thousands of people have suffered unimaginable horrors and have lost everything; dozens have lost their lives.

Perhaps Dawn is right; perhaps the men who have raped, looted, burned, tortured and murdered will get their comeuppance in the months and years ahead. Perhaps the woman manning the Air Zimbabwe information desk on the night Dawn begged to use a telephone, the Zimbabwean police who have turned their backs for almost two years, the men who attacked and raped Dawn, will not be able to sleep at night. Perhaps they have made their own hell for themselves.

I am indebted to Dawn for allowing me to tell her story, because she has taught me a lot about myself. Every letter from her closes with the words 'Oceans of Peace'. Her journey back from the brink has begun and her courage and strength will hopefully help others. She has given a face and a voice to the hundreds of women who have been raped in Zimbabwe under the guise of 'land redistribution'. Rape, an unacceptable crime under any circumstances, was made even worse when the perpetrators were able to get away with their crimes because of their political affiliations. Dawn speaks for all who have been unable to do so for themselves.

SIX

HOME INVASIONS AND OTHER VIOLATIONS

'This is my farm. This is my fields. This is my ostriches. This is my house. You get out by 4.00 pm. This is my house.'

These words had been spat at me by war veterans at my farm gate in 2000. Now what we had all thought were idle threats became reality in June 2001 for dozens of farmers in Zimbabwe. Farm invasions had become an everyday event, then there were company invasions, and now, the final indignity, the attempted takeover of homes. The madness was mounting; the police continued to do nothing and the government refused to intervene as mobs of marauding militants went around the country attempting to evict farmers from their homes. The tactics used were crude and obscene, the intimidation and harassment were extreme. Putting a personal face on it was not hard when I got a phone call one night from a farmer in Macheke. He was at his wits' end and told me exactly what was happening on his son Mike's nearby farm.

Shortly before midnight 25 men had arrived at the locked gate in the security fence surrounding Mike's farmhouse. They were determined to get inside and had weakened the gate on their last three visits in recent weeks. The men had tied ropes from the gate to a vehicle and attempted to rip it open. They had rammed into it and the mesh was dented, broken in places and roughly patched. On this night they succeeded and, under the glare of the security lights, they finally pushed open the gates and stormed into Mike's garden.

Farmers' names have been changed to protect them and their families – the events related are factual.

The men had already been into the village where Mike's farm workers lived and forced ten employees to come and join them. They were going to have an all-night party, known as a *pungwe*, on Mike's lawn in an attempt to scare him and his young family so much that they would leave – and then the war veterans could take over his house. Mike's four German Shepherd dogs had been cowed into silence and would do nothing as the invaders lit a large fire on the lawn.

Drumming on tins, shouting, singing, chanting and ululating, the war veterans partied on into the night. Mike, his wife Rose, and their three children, all under ten, got out of bed, switched on the lights and huddled together. They were hugely outnumbered, the children were already crying and Mike did not dare leave his family, did not dare go out. He called on the farm radio to his neighbours and phoned the police and then he just sat and listened to the madness one thin wall away from him and his family. He could do nothing except wait for someone to come and help; he could not even protect his own wife and children.

Mike knew the man leading the war veterans. He was known as the Base Commander and had been told repeatedly that Mike's farm, although listed for government seizure, was in the process of being de-listed. The Base Commander was not interested in hearing this or seeing any of Mike's paperwork or legal letters. This was an extremely productive farm and the Base Commander wanted it and Mike's house for himself. For weeks he had been harassing Mike, intimidating the workers and doing everything he could to wear the farmer down, tip him over the edge so that he would pack up and leave. The Base Commander knew that even if the police did come out to the farm, they would not arrest him; he was above the law, he was the law.

When the men in the garden saw the lights go on in the house they increased the noise and when no one came out, they stepped up the intimidation. Stones, rocks and sticks pelted onto the roof, more fires were lit closer to the house, and the invaders' dogs barked, howled and squabbled as they raced around Mike's garden.

Inside the house Mike and Rose were struggling to calm and reassure their children, who were terrified, crying and whimpering. It was almost impossible to find the words to tell them that everything would be all right, that the men in the garden would go away and that the police would soon come. Rose knew these things were unlikely to happen and she struggled to stop her own hands from trembling, battled to keep her tears at bay as she sat comforting her children. She feared for them all, for their lives and safety, and prayed for dawn and sanity.

Rose feared also for her children's minds. Her five-year-old son was already showing signs of distress. He was quiet and withdrawn and was often unwell lately, with increasing headaches, a recurring sore throat and earache. The doctors could not find anything physically wrong with him, but the psychological effects of prolonged stress were as clear as day.

A little before one in the morning the police arrived at Mike's farm. They did not order the Base Commander and his mob to leave, make them get out of the garden or extinguish their fires. They did not even charge the mob with breaking down Mike's gate – because the Base Commander and his midnight revellers ordered the police to leave. The police did not get to the house to speak to Mike and his wife; they were there for less than ten minutes and told neighbouring farmers that they were outnumbered and would return in the morning. Later in the night the Police Support Unit arrived at the farm, but they too retreated, saying they were outnumbered and would come back in the daytime.

Mike, Rose and their three children were alone. The *pungwe* carried on all night, and when dawn finally arrived they were not allowed out of their own house. The Base Commander had posted watchers at every door and Mike would have to wait for a politician to be summoned – the Base Commander would listen only to a politician.

Closing Mike's story, in an article I wrote for the *Zimbabwe Independent*, I found it hard to comment on this horror without anger: 'What is happening on Zimbabwe's farms is not about land. The 25 war veterans having a *pungwe* outside a farmers' bedroom window in the middle of the night are not landless peasants. These men throwing rocks on roofs, shouting, chanting and singing do not want to be farmers. These men want what other people have got. They want our homes, our possessions and our livelihoods. They do not want to 'liberate' land stolen from their ancestors, they want the good life and they are taking it. They are being allowed to take it and day after day, night after night, we are letting them get away with it ... This is not fiction, it is happening every single day and we are allowing it to continue.'

With complete anarchy the order of the day on hundreds of farms in Zimbabwe, violence, beating and torture almost daily occurrences in rural centres and villages, we all wondered what would happen when it was announced that Chenjerai 'Hitler' Hunzvi was dead. The infamous 51-year-old leader of the War Veterans Association died on 4 June 2001. The government and state media said that he had died of malaria, but the gossip and rumour that it was in fact Aids was widespread. Hunzvi was the third Member of Parliament to die in the last two months; the fifth in the past year.

President Mugabe, clearly shocked, spoke immediately about Hunzvi's role in land redistribution and his words, wreathed in rhetoric, were worrying in the extreme.

'Predictably Comrade Hunzvi was demonised and disparaged by a hostile and vicious local and international campaign that sought, and still does, to preserve the iniquitous colonial land ownership imbalance in Zimbabwe. Unfortunately his untimely death has come when victory of the ongoing land-based Third Chimurenga was now in sight. There can be no greater tribute and honour to him than that of an intensified campaign.' (*Chimurenga* means a militant revolt or rebellion against colonial or white people. The first had been the Ndebele uprising against pioneers, the second was the war for independence and the land evictions came to be known as the third.)

None of the usual protocol was followed in deciding on the hero status of Chenjerai Hunzvi. President Mugabe simply declared that he was a national hero; his remains would be buried in Heroes Acre and a full state funeral would be accorded him. This decision caused anger and scorn and the highly respected nationalist leader James Chikerema said: 'I cannot even comment on the issue because the concept of conferring hero status is being used for political mileage by Zanu PF.' Outspoken political analyst Masipula Sithole said: 'They are making the Heroes Acre a Zanu PF graveyard. It is no longer the Heroes Acre of Herbert Chitepo, Jason Moyo, Josiah Tongogara and other genuine heroes.'

In the days between the death and burial of Chenjerai Hunzvi – who was given a full state funeral and buried in a pure white casket at Heroes Acre – the eulogies were prolific, many government officials using the occasion to lash out at the people of the country. The Minister of Information, Jonathan Moyo, referred to whites as being non-African and blacks supporting the MDC as 'modern-day Uncle Toms' for not mourning his death.

Perhaps Minister Moyo also regarded black commercial farmers who did not support Zanu PF or their land policies as 'modern-day Uncle Toms'. A black farmer had his Chegutu property seized by war veterans. Philemon Matibe, the MDC candidate for Chegutu, was given seven days to vacate his property by war veterans – and if there were still any disbelievers about the real facts behind land redistribution, Matibe's case was absolute proof that it was only about politics. Matibe had lost the parliamentary election to Zanu PF's Webster Shamu, and was contesting the results.

As the date for the electoral contest drew near, pressure mounted on Matibe to withdraw his court challenges, and when he did not do so, his farm was taken over. A group of war veterans, led by the Chegutu District Administrator and a policeman, arrived on the farm and started allocating pieces to people they claimed were landless peasants. The invaders informed Matibe that he and the 100 workers he employed had seven days to vacate the property or face unspecified action. Philemon Matibe vacated his property and instituted legal proceedings to sue the government. In a statement to the press, he said: 'In essence what the government is saying is that I am not entitled to own land in Zimbabwe. But I am a black person and the government's land reform programme is meant to empower indigenous people.'

Regardless of Jonathan Moyo's propaganda that whites were sell-outs and blacks non-African, the evidence on the ground every day revealed more and more examples of unity amongst Zimbabweans, and of people, regardless of their colour, helping one another survive these horrific days. I got a call one evening from a white farmer who, with a couple of others, had gone to the rescue of nine black security guards who had been abducted by war veterans. The story he related was one of hundreds that made a nonsense of the government's rhetoric about racism, white superiority and black sell-outs.

A gang of men using the name of war veterans arrived at the bar of the Macheke Hotel and in full view of the patrons they abducted a man and ordered him to take them, in his car, to a remote country road. Arriving at their destination, the war veterans dumped their captor on the side of the road and, taking his vehicle, went to a building that housed the Macheke farm security guards. Nine off-duty guards were in the building when the veterans arrived. Two guards were assaulted and left bleeding on the floor and the other seven were forced into a vehicle and taken away. Arriving back in Macheke town, the war veterans took their prisoners to a public bar where they hauled them out and beat them publicly in front of many witnesses before taking them to the edge of a remote communal land. Here the seven men were again beaten, kicked and berated for working for white people. The seven guards, outnumbered by more than four to one, were helpless to even defend themselves and were left lying in the dust in the middle of the night when their captors finally tired of them.

Meanwhile, the first two guards who had been left behind at the base managed to raise the alarm and called for assistance. Five commercial farmers immediately went out in the cold and the dark to see what they could do to help. The first priority was to get medical assistance for the two beaten guards. One needed hospital care and the farmers took him to the police station for assistance. The police looked at the bleeding, groaning man, expressed sympathy, but said they had insufficient manpower to help. The farmers arranged for the man to be taken to hospital privately and asked the police to accompany them into the neighbourhood to look for the other seven abducted guards. Again the police expressed their sympathy but said they could not help until they had cleared it with their superiors.

The farmers were alone, without protection or assistance, but they did not give up and go home. They went out into the night to look for the abducted guards. The grass lining the roads was tall and dry; visibility was restricted to the beams of the headlights. It was eerie and frightening, never knowing what would be around the next corner, whether the next bend would find the road ambushed or laid with branches or rocks or lined with war veterans who were above the law. The search went on for three hours until all the guards were found and taken for medical treatment. Neither the farmers nor the guards wanted their names mentioned; they did not want to talk about what had happened, or who the attackers were. They feared that if they did, the perpetrators would be back.

As I had done so many times before, I wrote the article as accurately as possible, leaving out details that could identify the place or the people, and again closed with words of both anger and despair at a country whose people were paralysed by fear. 'Zimbabweans across the country have come to accept this. We are all filled with despair and frustration. We throw our hands up and say: "This shouldn't be happening" and we do nothing, say nothing. It is happening though, every day and every night. The people that grow our food are under attack.'

This one incident in Macheke was representative of the situation on farms and in rural areas around the country. With no foreign journalists allowed into the country and the local press repeatedly under attack anywhere outside the urban centres, it was these remote areas that continued to bear the brunt of the problems. Perhaps the government thought that out of sight meant out of mind, but the reports continued to come in via a variety of sources ranging from farm radios to e-mails and occasional newspaper reports. In the small area of Macheke alone, 16 000 farm workers faced unemployment and destitution as war veterans and militants disrupted farming operations and prevented farmers from planting or tending their crops.

Philip Munyanyi, general secretary of the Agricultural Workers Union, said that his organisation had tirelessly lobbied the government to give land to farm workers, to no avail. Speaking to the *Independent*, Munyanyi said: 'Farm workers are not being given land. No attention is being paid to their needs. It is a disastrous situation. They are just creating poverty.' It was becoming more and more obvious that it was the intention of invaders and war veterans to get farmers to leave their land, at almost whatever cost.

In Macheke a mob of 100 people arrived on a farmer's property and set fire to his tobacco seedbeds. Tobacco seedlings are grown in fumigated, sanitised beds, protected with mulch and surrounded by grass shelters to protect them from wind and inclement weather. The burning of these seedbeds, according to the farmer, meant a loss of over 300 acres of tobacco, to the value of Z$42 million – all of which would have been in foreign currency so vital for the economy's survival. Burning seedbeds was vindictive economic sabotage and took place on seven farms around the country in the space of less than a week.

In Masvingo, war veterans were seriously disrupting operations, and the regional chairman of the Commercial Farmers Union, Mike Clark, began warning how serious the situation was and what the implications for the future would be. Speaking to reporters from the *Daily News*, Mike said that wheat had only been planted on 80 hectares of land in his area as compared to the 600 hectares under the crop in the previous season. War veterans damaged irrigation equipment, stole piping and vandalised risers and sprinklers. 'Irrigation equipment worth more than Z$10 million has been vandalised on commercial farms where sugar cane and wheat are grown. The situation is unbearable and production on some properties has stopped.'

With reports like this coming in every week, serious food shortages in the months and even years ahead were inevitable, but agriculture Minister Dr Joseph Made continued to insist that there would be no shortages and everything was as it should be on the country's farms. He said he had surveyed production from the air: 'There is no need for the government to import any maize. It is absolutely untrue that we will import maize. I have flown around the country and seen that there is plenty of maize in the communal and resettlement areas. I am confident no one will starve, since maize is there.'

Minister Made said nothing about wheat, sugar, tobacco, livestock or any of the other crops war veterans were preventing farmers from planting or tending, and the results of his aerial survey were highly dubious. The implications for food security for Zimbabwe could only be dire – but no one in the government was taking any notice at all of warnings pouring in from every quarter. Our government was a willing accomplice to what would inevitably be widespread hunger and even starvation, and did not seem to care at all about the thousands of black people employed on commercial farms. It apparently did not even care about murder.

Zondiwa Dumukani, a 32-year-old driver employed on Blackfordby Farm in Harare, was beaten repeatedly by war veterans wielding axes, sticks and a golf club. Zondiwa, accused of not attending a Zanu PF rally, was brutally assaulted and died even though there was a heavy police presence and a ZBC television crew on the farm at the time. His murder made front-page news in the Independent papers but as always there was no comment from government officials and no arrests were made, despite eyewitnesses having named three of the assailants. The suffering and pain of ordinary Zimbabweans had become completely inconsequential in the quest for political survival.

The government tightened up on the few British journalists still operating in the country and in June expelled all they could find. Amongst these were Sean Langan, a BBC documentary producer, David Blair, a writer for the UK *Daily Telegraph*, and a BBC crew including Simon Finch, John Sweeney and James Miller. All were told they were no longer welcome in the country and had their entry permits withdrawn for one reason or another. The pressure on those of us Zimbabweans still getting information out of the country became almost unbearable and my days were largely spent on the telephone and e-mail, fingers flying across the keyboard.

News came in that war veterans had invaded the Beatrice Country Club, expelled the members and taken over the premises. The invasion came after a cricket match that war veterans said farmers had held to celebrate the death of Chenjerai Hunzvi. Twenty men took over the premises, drank all the beer in the fridges, consumed all the food in the freezers, wrote Zanu PF slogans on the walls and erected a sign in the driveway that read: 'Hitler Club. Chenjerai Hunzvi.' Police did nothing as the revellers lit fires on the lawn, lowered a boom across the driveway and held nightly parties at the club. It seemed there was no limit to the crimes you could get away with if you called yourself a war veteran and swore allegiance to Zanu PF.

The police continued to do nothing, using the word 'political' to excuse their inaction. Even when the police did react to a farmer's call for help, they appeared powerless. When a mob of 50 youngsters arrived at Johan's gate he was at home with Betty, his 78-year-old mother. Betty had been on this Beatrice farm for 55 years and her son for the last two decades. Johan had had visits from war veterans and farm invaders before. His highly productive maize and cattle farm had originally been listed for government acquisition in 2000, but he had gone to the courts, appealed against the designation and won his case. The farm had been de-listed months before – and then, in June 2001, it was again listed for government seizure.

Johan employed 25 permanent workers and up to 200 seasonal employees during the maize reaping season. He, his wife Mary Jane and their two children were all born in Zimbabwe, and this was the only farm they owned. Luckily Mary Jane and the two children were not on the farm when the mob of agitated men arrived at the gate.

'Get out!' the men shouted at Johan. 'You have 30 minutes to pack your things and get off this farm.'

'You are many,' Johan replied calmly, 'but I am one man. You must do what you have to do but I am staying here.'

This statement incensed the war veterans and they immediately started shouting and chanting.

'I am going to the house to phone the police,' Johan said, turning his back on the men at the gate and walking back towards his house. The noise and shouting behind him increased to fever pitch and by the time he reached the house the mob had broken through his gates and were coming across the garden towards him. Hurriedly Johan got his two Labradors and locked himself inside. He phoned both the police and neighbouring farmers for assistance.

When the police came they told Johan to stay calm and not to lose his temper or make demands. They said they did not have the authority to remove the men from his garden because the matter was 'political', but that the numbers present would decrease and that he would be allowed more freedom as time passed.

For five days and nights Johan and his elderly mother could not leave their house. The men camped out in their garden, lit fires on the lawn and demanded that Johan provide firewood and maize meal. For most of the day they lounged on Johan's garden furniture, built great bonfires on the lawns and tended pots of bubbling sadza. At dusk when the temperature dropped the men would move their fires closer to the house. The smoke curled between gaps in the walls, wisped through ventilation blocks and under doors.

As night fell the men would step up the intimidation. They drummed, ululated, sang, chanted and whistled, their aim being to intimidate and wear Johan down so that he would leave and they could move into his home. The men in the garden took turns and worked in relays going round and round the house, banging on doors and windows, drumming on tins and milk cans and throwing rocks and missiles onto the roof throughout the night.

Along with dozens of other people I phoned Johan every day to see how he was. Mostly he was tired. He said the constant noise was utterly exhausting. It went on and on, and he and his mother struggled to sleep or concentrate on anything as the incessant banging filled their senses and battered their minds. For five days and nights Johan and his mother were barricaded into their home until at last a neighbour negotiated with a politician to get the men moved out of Johan's garden. For five days and nights this farmer, a born and bred Zimbabwean, had refused to give these mobsters his home while his mother, the same age as our President, bravely endured the invaders' noise, taunts, smoke and terror.

When at last it was over Johan sent out a letter of thanks to everyone who had supported him. His closing words left me with a deep feeling of sadness and despair about the future of our country. 'I am feeling very depressed and on the verge of crying. There seems to be no hope for us white people and for the many good black people threatened by the coming collapse of our farming sector. Living in Zimbabwe we have come to accept that experiences such as ours are normal. What is our country coming to?'

The most shocking blow yet to commercial agriculture in Zimbabwe came on 29 June 2001. The *Herald* newspaper published a monstrous supplement of farms to be acquired by the government. It ran to 18 pages, listed over 2 000 properties – and appeared to signal an end to the last remnants of food security in Zimbabwe.

SEVEN

NO-GO AREA FOR WHITES

With the arrival of summer 2001 came the start of a new campaign of terror. People squatting on farms and others who had supposedly been allocated plots of land began to get restless as the growing and rainy season approached. The farmers too were getting desperate, with no clear directive from anyone on how to progress. The messages coming through from the official government departments conflicted with rulings made by the High and Supreme Courts. Farmers were winning their objections to compulsory acquisition and having their properties de-listed, but this was a mere technicality to the people squatting on farms or to the politicians on the ground.

A court order would say the farmer's land was not wanted by government and that he could continue farming, but this would not be implemented by district or provincial administrators, who continued to say that the farms were to stop operating and no food should be grown. Sometimes, when both courts and politicians agreed that a farmer should be left alone, a war veteran, mob of youths or even an arbitrary man on a bicycle could stop all work and cause terror on a farm. In all cases police refused to get involved in removing squatters from farms, saying it was a political matter and they would not assist in enforcing or upholding court rulings. In some cases farmers took out eviction notices against squatters who would not leave, but when the Messenger of the Court tried to serve papers, he was chased away and assaulted.

Trying to keep track of it all was almost impossible, but this particular bout of summer madness appeared to begin on a farm just outside Mutare. According to a widely distributed e-mail, which was supported by the Commercial Farmers Union, a Mutare farmer knocked down and killed Phibian Mapenzautswa shortly after the farmer drove onto a main road that ran through his farm. There were a large number of people on both sides of the road, many of whom were war veterans and farm occupiers. A petrol tanker was approaching from the opposite direction and as Mr Bezuidenhout passed it a man stepped out from behind the tanker and directly into the path of the farmer's car. Because there were so many people on the road, many of whom reacted angrily to the accident, Mr Bezuidenhout did not stop but drove straight to the police station to make a report. The people on the roadsides later alleged that Mr Bezuidenhout had deliberately run down and killed Mr Mapenzautswa, and war veterans in the area went on the rampage.

Three farms owned by Mr Bezuidenhout and his brothers were broken into by armed men who smashed windows, doors and computers, looted televisions, electrical equipment and clothing and left a trail of destruction. War veterans issued an order to all farmers in the area to immediately vacate their properties, which many did amidst reports of armed mobs travelling through the district. A senior war veteran in Harare announced on ZBC television: 'This is a revolution. This is the time to show the white minority that we are very angry and they must leave immediately.' The Minister of Information, Jonathan Moyo, described the accident as a 'callous, cold-blooded, premeditated murder which smacks of the Ku Klux Klan type of murders done in the US and South Africa.' The government, war veterans and state media had tried, convicted and sentenced Mr Bezuidenhout before any charges had been laid or lawyers consulted. ZBC TV showed the police taking the farmer to the scene of the accident, barefoot, in handcuffs and leg irons. Mr Bezuidenhout's lawyer was harassed and chased away from the area when he tried to take statements and when the farmer appeared in front of a magistrate the courtroom was filled with armed riot police and war veterans.

In the midst of all the mayhem surrounding the car accident, few people seemed to appreciate the tragic irony surrounding the identity of the deceased man. Thirty-one-year-old Phibian Mapenzautswa, described by the state media as a 'settler farmer', was apparently being allocated a piece of land at the time of the accident.

Mr Mapenzautswa was not a landless peasant; he was an accountant, employed as a finance manager at the huge Mutare Board and Paper Mills company. He was gainfully employed, earning a higher than average income and residing in a city. By no stretch of the imagination was the deceased man a landless peasant; he was too young to have been in the war of liberation and had both education and employment to his credit. The death of Mr Mapenzautswa was tragic, but so were the political circumstances that had allowed a qualified accountant to be classed as a landless peasant. Mr Mapenzautswa should not have died – but then he should not have allowed himself to be used for political purposes.

Shortly after the incident in Mutare, in early August, a farmer in Kwekwe was murdered. Seventy-six-year-old Ralph Corbett was attacked in his own home by suspected war veterans and government supporters. Telephone lines to the farmhouse had been cut and the attackers apparently tied Mr Corbett up with electrical cable before axing him in the head, causing severe brain damage, which led to his death a few days later. A news report from South Africa quoted one of Mr Corbett's daughters as saying that her father had agreed to let war veterans stay on the farm on condition that he be allowed to stay in the farmhouse until his death. An official statement from the Commercial Farmers Union, though, said that the murder was probably not connected to either land invasions or war veterans who had been squatting on Mr Corbett's farm for many months. If that was the case, it was hard to understand why, apart from one handgun, nothing had been taken from Mr Corbett's home of 50 years.

Before the funeral of Ralph Corbett had even taken place in Kwekwe, war veterans and government supporters went on an orgy of looting on farms in and around Chinoyi. For the first time in two years, farmers defended themselves and clashed with settlers and war veterans. Everyone wondered how farmers had kept their tempers for so long and put up with so much, but they had. They all knew that as whites we had few rights in Zimbabwe; as farmers we had even fewer. The restraint of white farmers even in the face of murder, torture, abduction and destruction was a quality that set them aside from anyone else in the country.

Approximately forty war veterans and farm occupiers armed with axes, fence poles and rocks stormed the house on Liston

Shields farm in Chinoyi, owned by Tony Barklay. Tony locked himself in one room of the house and as the invaders began hammering on the doors to get in, he called for assistance from both police and neighbouring farmers. The police reported that they did not have transport to attend the farm and they refused assistance from neighbouring farmers who offered to go and collect them. When pressed, the police finally agreed to send a detail on a bicycle from the nearest police base, which was 20 kilometres away from Tony's home. Farmers told the police that it would take at least two hours for the detail to travel the distance on a bicycle, but the police said that was their final decision.

Meanwhile, six farmers arranged to go to Tony's assistance while another continued phoning other police officials for help. A woman superintendent was told that six farmers were going to Tony's assistance and she promised to have the support unit mobilised immediately. The support unit did not arrive at the farm. When Tony no longer answered the repeated calls on his radio, farmers agreed to try to approach the mob at the door and negotiate for his release. Two of them approached the settlers but were immediately attacked with bricks, rocks, catapults and branches. The farmers retreated and discussed amongst themselves what to do. They decided that they must try to get Tony out of his house. This decision resulted in a confrontation between farmers and war veterans, leaving five people injured on either side, but the farmers gained access to the house and rescued Tony.

Later in the afternoon police finally went out to the farm. A number of war veterans were picked up and farmers were asked to accompany the police to the station so that a report could be made. The farmers agreed, but instead of being asked to make reports on the incident they were all immediately arrested. Later in the afternoon friends and relatives of the farmers went to the police station to find out what was happening and what the charges were. They too were arrested, including a 72-year-old man who had gone to the station with blankets.

The following morning another farmer from the area went to the police station to try and find out on what charges all these people were being detained. While he was there a marked government vehicle drove into the station and four men got out and entered the police base. These men insisted that this farmer also be arrested –

and arrested he was, despite having been in a meeting with one of the police inspectors at this very same police station at the time of the incident. The inspector threw his hands up and did nothing.

Twenty-two farmers were now in custody. All had been ordered to remove their outer clothing and shoes; they were not allowed to receive the food, clothing or blankets bought by their relations and were not given anything to eat for the first 24 hours. There was no furniture of any kind in the cells and the men lay on scraps of torn blanket on the cement floors. Eight men in a cell shared three blankets. An identification parade was held at which farm settlers and war veterans were only able to identify seven of the 22 men – and three of the seven had not even been on the farm at the time of the incident the previous day. After the identification parade the men were given a communal bowl of maize porridge and a small plate of about 150 grams of dried fish to share between them all. After the men had eaten they were loaded into three police vehicles and told they were being taken out to the farm for a further identification parade. Half-way to the farm the plan changed and the men were returned to police cells.

The first intimation I had of this nightmare was an e-mail from a farming friend in Chinoyi who knew of my writing and the size of my e-mail address book. 'Twenty-one farmers have been arrested in Chinoyi. They have been stripped of their shoes and jackets and have no access to blankets. Not only that but anybody who has tried to help has also been arrested or beaten up ... This is not a land issue, it is totally political. The farmers have no protection and anyone who helps ends up beaten or arrested ... Please let the world know what is going on in Zimbabwe. Love Mandy.'

Mandy's request for help was desperate and with it came dozens of other reports detailing escalating violence in Chinoyi. Kerry, a friend in Marondera, drove through to Chinoyi to try and help friends who were involved and she soon found herself entangled in the political mayhem ravaging Chinoyi. She went with the wife of one of the arrested farmers to the Chinoyi police station at eight in the morning. The police camp yard was crowded with young government supporters. Entering the charge office, Kerry found a 76-year-old doctor who had just arrived at the police station to offer treatment to the prisoners. The doctor had been assaulted by the youths with a bicycle chain at the station gate in front of policemen.

His glasses were broken and there was both internal and external bleeding of his eye. His son had also been assaulted in the police camp grounds by youths with sticks, as was the wife of another arrested farmer.

Kerry, an ex-policewoman herself, watched in horror as the police refused to accept a Report of Assault from the elderly doctor. Kerry asked the police to give her a Medical Report Form but they refused. By this time a number of the government youths had entered the charge office and Kerry advised the doctor and farmers' wives to leave immediately. When they went out into the car park they found the tyres on their vehicles had been deflated. Flat tyres or no, they all fled into the nearby town of Chinoyi and headed for safety.

The incident at the Chinoyi police station was just the beginning, as more government youths entered the town, massed in the streets, stoned cars carrying white people and attacked shoppers at random. A 72-year-old white woman standing in a queue at the post office was pushed around and slapped. Another woman in her sixties was jostled and rammed with a trolley while standing in a supermarket. A 45-year-old man was chased down the street, kicked, beaten, punched and stabbed twice. A 50-year-old man was badly beaten with sticks as he walked down the main street of the town. A black man was pulled out of a car being driven by a white and hit before being told not to travel with whites.

The trouble in the town was only the tip of the iceberg as government supporters proceeded into the farming area, ransacking, looting and trashing homesteads. At Two Trees Farm near Lions Den, a mob of men barricaded a farmer, his wife and their two daughters, one of whom was an eight-month-old baby, into their home. Through the window the farmer could see his workshop being looted, but could do nothing. He watched in horror as a mob stormed his security fence, broke down the gate and fired a shot. He went outside and saw that his dog had been shot, but had to retreat into his house when someone fired a shot at him. Finally released after seven hours, the farmer was ritually humiliated by two government ministers and the Provincial Governor in front of state-owned television cameras. He was accused of having shot his own dog, and ordered to live in peace with the men squatting on his property.

One of these government ministers was filmed by Channel 4 as he addressed the government youths and settlers. In Shona, the

Minister said: 'If you get hold of MDC supporters, beat them until they are dead. Burn their farms and their worker's houses, then run away fast and we will then blame the burning of the workers' houses on the whites. Report to the police because they are ours.' The film footage caused a storm, the government minister denied that he had ever said the words captured on the video footage, but the squatters, settlers and youths did indeed go on the rampage through Chinoyi. Squatters and youths piled farm equipment, fertiliser and household possessions onto looted tractors and trailers. Over two dozen farmers evacuated their properties as more than twenty farms were looted. One of the farms looted belonged to Mandy, who had alerted me to the situation. She wrote as a refugee from a friend's house and her letters were heartbreaking.

'Nothing prepared me for what I saw – as a friend of mine said, this is the work of the Antichrist. Absolutely everything had gone, including the roof and window frames. All that was left were the walls. The only thing lying on the floor was a serviette ring that my daughter had used at school. Even our cat had not been spared, they shot her with a shotgun, there were cartridges all over the house. They then stripped the lemon trees and the vegetable garden. Our workers were forced to attend a *pungwe* while they ransacked.'

Mandy's horror was the same for more than twenty other families whose properties were completely stripped by looters. BBC reporters witnessed huge looting of fertiliser and household goods. Light fittings were smashed out of walls, books were burned and a piano smashed. Water taps were opened and left running and they described the scene as a sea of water and paper. Reporters said cows were slaughtered and loaded onto stolen tractors and trailers, fires were started in workers' villages and farm workers were assaulted if they did not help load looted belongings. An estimated 8 000 people, including farmers and their workers, were affected and damage was estimated at a conservative 500 million dollars.

When the 23 arrested farmers were due to appear in front of a magistrate the hearing had to be postponed as a mob of government supporters threatened to kill them if they were granted bail. The magistrate called off the remand hearing and ordered the farmers be held in custody because of the chanting militants outside the court room.

Many of the farmers who had evacuated their properties were unable to return to their homes for days as militants felled trees which they used to block roads. It took some days before even the SPCA could go in to rescue domestic animals and ensure that cattle and other livestock had water. Dozens of men in Chinoyi shaved their heads in sympathy and support of their countrymen who had their heads shaved whilst in prison. The arrested farmers were all charged with public violence and spent two weeks in prison. They were finally released on unheard-of conditions, which included: Z$100 000 cash surety, Z$100 000 assurity and the surrendering of their passports. In addition they were barred from the district for four weeks and had to report to a police station every Friday.

The reaction by Zimbabweans to the looting in Chinoyi and the arrests of farmers and bystanders was one of immediate horror. Many black Zimbabweans wrote to newspapers expressing their feelings of anger and many wrote to me saying how disgusted they were at what everyone saw and called ethnic cleansing. My mother, Pauline Henson, who had fought most of her life for an end to racism and who chose to live as the only white person in a completely black town, wrote a poem which was published in the *Daily News* and which said it all.

White Africans
White Africans don't need a yellow star
for you to know just who they are.
They don't need that badge of shame
for you to know just who to blame
for what they did
(one hundred years ago and more)

'The men with no knees'
that's what people called them when they came.
Grabbing land and laying claim
to all, in Queen and country's name.
They're the ones who stole the land
back when CJ and his 'gallant' band
came rolling up across the plains
with their bibles – and their rifles – and their wagon trains
(one hundred years ago and more)

But that was then – this is now.
Shall we live forever in the shadow of the past?
Blaming, shaming, holding on to hate
to see it stay and sour all our days?
Their children and their children's children
must they forever pay?
(one hundred years ago and more)

The state-run radio and television coverage of the entire Chinoyi mayhem was unbelievable. White farmers were accused of looting their own farms and the Minister of Information, Jonathan Moyo, said that British diplomats had colluded with white farmers to destroy their own farms in order to discredit the government. The *Herald* newspaper stated that farmers had paid their own employees to loot and trash the farms. The *Daily News,* however, published the most graphic accounts of the looting of farms and on 14 August its front-page headline was 'Police vehicle used in farm looting spree.' This report led to the arrest of the editor and reporters from the newspaper.

The huge courage of the *Daily News* and its black reporters was not emulated by our farming leaders. In the midst of the mayhem the Commercial Farmers Union issued a bland press statement listing some of the millions of dollars' worth of property that had been looted or trashed. With 22 of its members in prison, 8 000 people homeless and two dozen properties destroyed, it closed its press release with these words: 'Meanwhile the CFU and its partners, driving the Zimbabwe Joint Resettlement Initiative (ZJRI), are committed to finding common ground and all meetings currently being held are devoted to securing consensus on the land reform programme despite the tense situation on the ground.' It seemed the CFU was still unable to do what so many people were now doing – to condemn utterly and unequivocally the happenings on the farms. The CFU continued to dialogue with the very people who were instigating the mayhem that was gradually obliterating its membership. Double-speak was the order of the day.

On 6 September the government of Zimbabwe signed the Abuja Agreement promising an end to violent land invasions, but like ZJRI, it was no more than a useless piece of paper. ZJRI was a proposal whereby farmers gave land, inputs and a revolving loan to the government for distribution to resettled farmers. A million hectares was given, the government was delighted – and yet its supporters continued to grab more land, stop farmers from growing or tending crops, and allow war veterans to beat farm workers. ZJRI did not abandon its project, did not say that clearly they had been used; instead they gave more land and continued to say they wanted to dialogue with the government.

Since February 2000 I had been trying to speak out on behalf of farmers but the CFU was adamant that farmers should not speak to the press and should not tell their stories. As the nightmare continued, though, more and more farmers became dissatisfied with their union leaders, but they did nothing to change things. Time after time occasions were lost when the CFU could have gained enormous public sympathy and action, but they did not, saying they feared retribution for their members. With every outrage on a farm, every murder, torture or looting, the CFU made statements that were weak and totally inadequate. They reduced the number of farm situation reports from daily to three and then two times a week. They tagged on the end of their e-mails a disclaimer saying that the points made in the official CFU reports were private opinions and they would not be held liable for them. Other dire e-mails, about how many farmers were no longer operational or how many thousands of hectares had not been planted, were headed with the notice – 'confidential, not for press release or publication'. Many women farmer friends, as disgusted as I was, started to tag disclaimers on their letters to me: my favourite tongue-in-cheek one read: 'All messages reflect my personal opinions.'

The situation within the CFU seemed very similar to that in Zanu PF – the Director had been in his position for well over a decade and all the CFU officials and members were expected to toe the line. Many branch leaders were totally unhappy with statements they had to make, but could or would do nothing to change things. At one CFU meeting where hundreds of farmers were present and desperate for answers from the Director of the CFU, the grumblings and complaints from the floor were numerous. A farmer asked from what date the 90-day eviction on a Section 8 notice became valid – the date the letter was served or the date on which the government had made the new 90-day pronouncement on evictions. A ten-minute lecture on grammar ensued, hinging on the word 'may', as the statement read 'the government might give a 90-day eviction'.

It seemed ludicrous that with High and even Supreme Court rulings being disregarded every day in Zimbabwe, the CFU leaders still pinned their hopes on legalities. Aside from grammar, we learnt nothing at that meeting – and the farmer still did not know whether to start packing up his life or to wait on the off-chance that 'may' would hold water in a court of law. When farmers asked their union officials if help with legal expenses might be given by the CFU, they were told this could only be forthcoming if it proved to be a 'test case'. When another asked what to do about 200 head of cattle penned into a very small paddock and being held there by war veterans, he was told to 'dialogue' with the invaders. We all knew that this was impossible; we had all tried it, and I wondered if the CFU officials had ever even seen a war veteran, let alone tried to engage him in conversation. We all left the meeting with the distinct impression that the senior officials in the organisation had very little knowledge of exactly what was going on outside their Harare offices. It did not make any sense at all, and on many, many occasions I wondered what sort of double-speak game the CFU may have been engaged in.

As the men in Chinoyi had shaved their heads in solidarity with their imprisoned countrymen, I pinned a small yellow ribbon to my shirt in silent protest at anarchy and in support of all the people suffering in Zimbabwe. None of us thought things could get much worse, and hundreds of women both in and outside Zimbabwe joined me in wearing a yellow ribbon. Little did I realise at the time how long I would have to wear the ribbon for – it became an integral part of my wardrobe.

When I'd been wearing the ribbon for a few days Richard asked me about it.

'It's my way of saying I'm not happy with the troubles in Zimbabwe,' I responded.

'Good, me too Mum!' was his comment.

Even a small child, it seemed, had eyes to see and ears to hear that all was not well in Zimbabwe.

When people ask me now what the yellow ribbon is for and I tell them, they respond by saying how brave I am to wear it in public. And this is the face of Zimbabwe today – people are too scared even to join a silent protest, even to pin an innocent yellow ribbon onto their collars.

EIGHT

CLOSE ENCOUNTERS WITH TERROR

On 25 November 2001 a young farming couple in Macheke invited friends and neighbours for lunch. It was a lovely day and mostly the talk was not about what was happening on the farms or in the country but about happier times. There was a lot of laughter and humour and perhaps twenty of us sat under a tree in the garden trying, just for this day, to be normal.

There was no one at the gathering who was living anything like a 'normal' life. Most of the guests lived on farms that had been squatted on by war veterans. Many were no longer allowed to farm their land, having been told that the fields belonged to the invaders and that the farmers were not to grow food. Three of the guests at the luncheon had been victims of extreme violence and torture at the hands of war veterans the previous year. There were a handful of young children at the gathering, and they scampered around with a football, had turns on a bicycle and made everything seem completely normal.

The lunch was superb and we sat with plates on our laps under the tree and managed for a few hours to forget the horrors of everyday life in Zimbabwe. I did not know many of the people at the lunch, but they seemed to know who I was. As always, I was wearing a small yellow ribbon pinned to my shirt, my silent protest at anarchy.

'I see you're still wearing your yellow ribbon,' commented a burly, red-cheeked man in his thirties.

'Oh yes! I'm not taking it off until this madness is over.'

'We used to wear them too,' he said, 'but what's the point?'

'I don't know, Alan, but at least it's a way of continually showing disapproval at anarchy.'

'We used to wear them all the time,' he said again before we changed the conversation to comparing ages and trying to decide which of us had most grey hairs. Alan was younger than me and I can't remember who we decided was the greyer of the two of us. It was cause for parting laughter, though, and I left early, wanting to get back to Marondera before dark.

Little did we know how quickly the euphoric glow of a happy and relaxed day with friends would be obliterated. Within a few hours Alan would be ambushed and shot in his own driveway, and life for him and his family would never be the same again.

Soon after dark Alan and Anthea Bradley and their two boys, Luke and Mitchell, left the farm where we had all been lunching. Thirty-two-year-old Anthea was driving, Alan sat in the front passenger seat with Mitchell on his lap and Luke lay sleeping on the back seat of their red double-cab truck. As Anthea drove down the driveway towards their farmhouse, she saw that the road ahead was blocked with tree branches. She slowed down and stopped a short distance from the roadblock, but did not switch off the engine. She could see someone partially hidden behind a tree and called out to him to remove the branches from the road so that they could pass.

Alan got out and repeated the request, standing between the car and the door. Then Anthea saw what she knew was the barrel of a gun, and realised this was an ambush. She saw the man raise the gun, and immediately called out to Alan to get back into the car. As her husband did so Anthea knew the only way she could go was forward, over the barricade. Pressing her foot down hard on the accelerator, she raced forward and two shots rang out. The noise was immediate and deafening – from the explosion of the bullets, the shattering of the window and from the two children, screaming and screaming.

One bullet hit the driver's side window, which collapsed into a million squares and fragments around Anthea and onto her lap. The bullet grazed both of her shoulders before hitting Alan, shattering into his upper right arm and chest. The main part of the bullet deflected downwards and broke four of Alan's ribs before fragmenting in his right lung. The second bullet hit the dashboard of the car, split up, and went into the engine. Both children were awake and screaming and Alan was bleeding profusely in the seat next to her. There was not a second to lose; no time to panic or scream. Anthea was completely in charge and had to make instant decisions.

Anthea knew she had to get clear of the farm immediately. She drove round the circular drive and past the front of her own home, stopping briefly to check on Alan, who was not answering her repeated calls to him. She switched on the interior car light and her husband stared up at her, his mouth open, his shirt covered in blood. She thought he was dead, but then heard him breathing. Vague memories of first aid began to come back to her and she knew that she had to get him to a hospital, fast. Stopping briefly at the farm village, where the workers had begun gathering, she quickly told them Alan had been shot, then drove away to the safety of friends and neighbours already racing to meet her.

The first anyone knew about the ambush and shooting was at 7.20 pm when Anthea began frantically calling from the radio in her car. Eighty kilometres away in Marondera we heard her calls for help on the farm radio as we sat around the supper table. Immediately friends and neighbours closest to Anthea began responding to her calls. Farmers in Macheke and Virginia had had other such emergencies in the last two years and their organisation, professionalism and calmness were astounding as they dealt first with the priorities and then the practicalities. There was no hysteria, no panic and no chaos.

All over the area men were dispatched into the night to check the roads for other ambushes, to arrange for immediate medical assistance and to secure the two extremely traumatised but unhurt children. An ambulance was sent from Marondera to meet Anthea on the road and radio messages came in from everywhere. A nurse came on the radio and calmly explained that the wound in Alan's lung must be plugged to try and hold the escaping air, and how it should be stoppered with a plastic bag.

Less than ten minutes after the ambush and shooting Anthea was met by her parents and neighbours closest to the scene. The children were taken hurriedly into the safe and loving arms of their grandparents. Alan, still bleeding profusely, was carried off by friends to meet the ambulance and Anthea followed with other friends. Dozens of people offered to give blood – and even in such a crisis there was humour from these amazing people.

'What blood group is he? Is it of the human variety?'

'I haven't got Aids, I'll give blood,' called one of the men who had been beaten to a pulp by war veterans a year before.

'Hey, wasn't Alan bitten by a dog the other day? He hasn't got rabies, has he?'

A couple of farmers rushed to the Macheke police station and refused to leave until armed police had gone to the ambush site, and then they offered to go to Marondera and collect the Police Dog Unit. Arrangements were made for a security company to come out with tracker dogs before dawn the following morning.

Some farmers located and dismantled other roadblocks that had been set up in the area by war veterans, and people immediately arranged to meet and escort people home who were still travelling on the dark and dangerous roads through Macheke and Virginia. Many farmers' wives called, offering beds and food; others arranged to phone the press and contact Alan and Anthea's relations in Harare. Farmers went out to the Bradley farmhouse, checked the area thoroughly, told all the workers on the farm what had happened, made sure the house was safe and secure and then waited for well over an hour in the dark for the police to arrive.

At Borradaile hospital in Marondera, doctors attempted to stabilise Alan, who had lost a lot an enormous amount of blood, but within a couple of hours it was clear that he would have to be transferred to a major hospital in Harare. Anthea's incredible bravery and immediate action had saved the lives of her husband and two children and although in deep shock, with shrapnel in her shoulders and covered in cuts from the broken glass, she managed to answer all the questions being thrown at her by police, CID, doctors and nurses at the hospital. She and Alan were finally dispatched to Harare not long before midnight. The last call that came through on the radio that evening was that Alan was doing as well as could be expected; he was not yet stable and his condition was critical.

The morning after the shooting Alan was still critical and the messages were sobering as, throughout the day, updates were given on his condition. He was on a respirator in the intensive care unit of a big Harare hospital, had had two blood transfusions, was heavily sedated and his temperature was fluctuating. Doctors feared an infection in his lung.

After four days in intensive care Alan was taken off the sedatives and given epidural painkillers. He remained on the respirator until 1 December, when doctors finally removed all the pipes from his throat, and for the first time he could talk to his wife. Blood continued to drain from his lung, but three days later the catheter and feeding tubes were removed and he was taken off epidurals so that he could embark on the intensive physiotherapy needed to clear his lungs. On 7 December, twelve days after he had been shot, Alan's lungs were finally declared free of fluid, the drain was removed and he was taken out of the intensive care unit and transferred to a private ward. From that point on his recovery was rapid: soon he was discharged and put under the care of a physiotherapist who helped him recover the use of his right arm.

A couple of days after the ambush and shooting, a friend and I went to have a look at the damage to the Bradleys' car. What we saw was absolutely terrifying: it was miraculous that only Alan had been hurt. The driver's side window had completely disintegrated and there were two bullet holes in the centre of the dashboard, angling downwards and exiting into the engine casing of the car. We thought that the man shooting must have either been very tall or standing on a rise to have shot through the side window and lodged the bullets at this angle. There was a small, circular impact point on the outside of the windscreen on the driver's side, which may have been made by another bullet. We thought at least three bullets, and perhaps four, had been fired at Alan and Anthea when they were ambushed on the night of 25 November 2001. All I could think, as I looked at the damage, was that they and their two children definitely had a guardian angel with them on that never-to-be-forgotten night.

Six months after the shooting, I met the Bradleys to find out how they all were, and, as with so many others I had met, I was amazed at their recovery and their lack of anger and bitterness. Alan's physical recovery had been long and slow. The muscle in his upper arm had not yet rebuilt and appeared withered and drooping. The damage to his arm had affected his hand and fingers and Alan said his handwriting was still barely legible. His lung, shrunk by a third, had recovered, but he had not yet done anything extremely strenuous to test his lung capacity. Anthea told me that their two sons seemed to have come to some sort of peace with what had happened that night six months before. At first the boys, both under ten, had been unable to sleep alone and they had both gone for counselling to help them get over the trauma.

The Bradleys told me what had happened to the man who had shot Alan. Unlike almost all other cases of violence involving war veterans on farms, the man who shot Alan Bradley had been arrested. He had confessed and been charged with three counts of attempted murder. Initially he was held in police custody, but was later released on Z$5 000 bail. This sum was ridiculously low for three counts of attempted murder in comparison to the 23 farmers in Chinoyi, charged with public violence and eventually granted bail of Z$200 000 each. Conditions were attached to the shooter's bail – one being that he was prohibited from setting foot on the Bradley farm. Barely five months after he had shot Alan Bradley, however, the man was back on their farm and police seemed reluctant to arrest him for breaching bail conditions.

Shortly after the horrors encountered by the Bradleys, I met another couple living just outside Marondera who had also lived through a never-to-be-forgotten night of terror. Louis and Rita, an elderly couple, were no strangers to the activities of war veterans, having had their farm occupied by squatters since July 2000. The stories they told of their 16-month invasion were much the same as those of hundreds of other farmers. They had encountered repeated work stoppages, which eventually led Louis to get a Peace Order from the local police barring war veterans and occupiers from interfering with farm activities. The Peace Order meant little to the squatters, though, particularly as police were seldom on hand to enforce it. The 60 employees on Louis's farm were evicted from their village by war veterans and for months had been living in an empty tobacco barn on a neighbouring farm.

At one point in the invasion Louis officially handed over 500 acres of his property to the squatters, giving them his blessing to farm on his land and hoping that this would enable him to resume normal farming operations without continual harassment. The invaders were content for a little while, but soon came back to Louis saying that the 500 acres he had given them were not suitable for their needs and demanding that he have those 500 acres and they have the land he was using.

When Louis refused, the war veterans and invaders barricaded him into his home, pushed his 400-strong herd of cattle into the homestead garden and ploughed up his fodder plantations with oxen. For two weeks the invaders would not allow Louis to let his cattle out to graze and he was forced to feed them on hay – a huge operation, requiring 100 bales every day. The squatters then burnt his stock of hay bales and refused to let him dip the cattle. For 16 months Louis and Rita had tried to continue farming, surviving each encounter with the war veterans, until suddenly everything changed.

One evening, the couple noticed people gathering outside the homestead gate as it got dark. They lit a big fire next to the security fence where some geese had laid eggs: from inside the house Rita could hear the goose eggs exploding from the heat. Shortly after 7.00 pm there was frantic barking at the back of the house, while someone knocked loudly on the front door. Rita went to the back door and Louis to the front to find out what was happening.

Looking out into the darkness, Rita heard a roar and then saw a sea of people break down the gates and swarm across the garden towards the house. They were bellowing and shouting, and Rita barely had time to slam and lock the door before the men were everywhere. Meanwhile Louis was at the front door and opened it to see one of his employees who had no time for explanations or niceties.

'They're coming,' he said, 'Quick, they're coming in!'

Louis and Rita had nowhere to run to, no way of getting out of their own home because in moments it was surrounded by about forty men who immediately began attacking the house. Windows were rattled, gutters banged and a steady and incessant thumping began on the back door. The noise was overwhelming and increased as heavy objects were thrown onto the asbestos roof. Rita immediately called out for help on the farm radio, shouting over the roar of noise, begging neighbours to call the police and get someone to come and help them.

Rita and Louis stood alone and helpless as the mob outside began hammering at the back door with heavy objects. The situation was deteriorating by the second and still the police did not come. As the back door began to yield to the pressure from outside, they retreated into the hallway and locked the interleading door behind them. The noise escalated as the invaders came into the house; someone was walking on the roof, smashing a steel fencing pole into the asbestos, trying to get in from above. Then the noise was of breaking glass as the men smashed every window in every room of the house. The windows were barred, but even that seemed not to deter the invaders, who threw and smashed steel garden furniture against the bars, trying to buckle them.

When Rita and Louis heard the hallway door being hammered on, they were forced to leave the farm radio connected to its base set and retreat into their bedroom, where they locked the door and waited for help. Their only lifeline with the outside world now was their cell phone, and again they called for help. Still the police did not come. Huddled in the bedroom, Louis saw an arm come through the broken window with a burning branch, setting the curtains on fire. Prepared for the worst, he had put buckets of water in every room and he quickly managed to douse the flames; then the couple just sat and waited for someone to come to their rescue. The noise that had gone on for over two hours died down a little, but Rita and Louis had no way of finding out what was going on.

When at last help came three hours later, at 10 pm, there were no sirens, arrests or handcuffs; instead the situation was 'defused' by political intervention. A neighbour had arrived with a senior war veteran and within minutes the mob had completely dispersed. A short while later the police finally arrived and Rita and Louis came out of their bedroom, in deep shock, frightened and thankful to be alive. They saw the ruin that had been their home. A plug had been put into a sink and the taps turned on. The lounge, pantry and dining room were completely flooded; carpets and furniture stood in five centimetres of water. The contents of the fridge and deep freeze – meat, milk, fruit, vegetables and bread – were gone. Plates, drinking glasses and flower vases were smashed and there was broken glass everywhere. Cutlery had been taken from the drawers, wire and tools from the garage, and someone had attempted to drain the petrol from their car. The television decoder, a hat and walking stick had disappeared, but were found later under a bush in the garden.

Louis's African Grey parrot, a family pet which Louis had taught to talk, had gone from its cage, the little door ripped off completely. As the couple stood trying to take in the destruction all around them Louis spotted the parrot. It was sitting in a pool of water under the dining room table, soaked and with feathers fluffed, quietly muttering and swearing to itself! Twenty-five geese had been stolen from the garden, and for that three men were arrested the following morning. For the destruction amounting to nearly half a million dollars' worth of damage, no one was arrested. For the empty fridge and deep freeze, the missing cutlery and tools – no one was arrested. For the breaking and entering and extreme intimidation – no one was arrested.

When Louis and Rita had finished telling me of their horror, it again helped to put my own problems in perspective. I asked them what they would do now, where they would go and if they had plans for the future. 'We haven't got a plan B,' said Rita. 'That farm is 40 years of our life. We haven't got anywhere to go to. It could have been worse; at least we are alive.'

'They just want to get us out, that's all they want,' Louis said, his eyes shining with a mixture of laughter and tears. 'I'm not leaving! I can't go somewhere and live off charity. It's all just trying to scare us off. If they want to pay me, then I'll get off!'

Tall, thin and with a determined look in her eyes, Rita said to me as we parted: 'We've got to have hope, Cathy, we've just got to have hope.'

These were sentiments being expressed by farmers all over the country. If the Zimbabwe government would just abide by its own laws, pay for the farms that it wanted and respect people's human and constitutional rights, the farmers would leave. Both Rita and Louis played down their entire ordeal; there was no drama or embellishment, just straight facts. Their horror was just another story amongst hundreds where mobs of youths, often hyped up on drugs and alcohol, used the most obscene tactics to intimidate the weakest targets.

As summer wore on and both the end of the year and presidential elections approached, political violence was a part of everyday life. It spread like wildfire through remote country areas, into densely populated areas of towns and cities: it was not safe anywhere. The country's second city, Bulawayo, exploded during November when a war veteran was abducted and later found buried in a shallow grave. As with so many other stories, there was far more to the murder of war veteran Cain Nkala than met the eye.

In the 2000 parliamentary elections David Coltart's election agent, Patrick Nabanyama, was abducted and disappeared, never to be seen again. The abductors were known and eventually apprehended, but the courts repeatedly remanded them out of custody. War veteran Cain Nkala was one of the men involved in the disappearance and presumed murder of Nabanyama. His next court appearance was due in February 2002 and sources told newspapers that Nkala had had enough and was about to spill the beans as to what had happened to Nabanyama and who was responsible.

Early in November Nkala was taken from his home in the middle of the night by ten men armed with Kalashnikov rifles. There was a scuffle, apparently, and his wife was slightly injured, but an immediate police and security ring was put around Mrs Nkala and although she was the only witness to her husband's abduction, she did not say a word and would not speak to the press. The state media, war veterans and government immediately blamed the MDC for the disappearance of Nkala.

Threats demanding his return came thick and fast. The MDC Harare offices were raided by a mob of 100 war veterans and government supporters, staff members and passers-by were assaulted and injured and cars passing the building were stoned and damaged. In Bulawayo armed police raided the MDC headquarters, ransacked the premises, saying they were looking for information regarding the disappearance of Nkala, and arrested security guards. A week later the body of Cain Nkala was found in a shallow grave just outside Bulawayo city. In one of the most obscene reports ever seen on the local media, two young MDC supporters were interrogated, and apparently confessed to the murder of the war veteran in front of ZBC television cameras, whilst policemen unearthed a partly decomposed limb.

Even with two youngsters having supposedly confessed to the crime, more than a dozen people were immediately arrested, including leading businessmen and an MDC Member of Parliament. ZBC television and the *Herald* newspaper carried the most outrageous, nonsensical allegations, which tried, convicted and sentenced the arrested men before they had even been charged. The arrested men were denied access to their lawyers for the first 48 hours and were not allowed to receive food, blankets or life-saving medication, including heart tablets and insulin.

One of the men arrested was a friend and I was devastated to see him in handcuffs on the front page of the *Herald*. At night, when I put Richard to bed, our bedside prayers were expanded when my son added the words: 'And look after Mummy's special friend in Bulawayo.'

The horror for those men and hundreds of people in Bulawayo extended into all our lives. Richard came home from school with an exercise book I had not seen before called Devotions. I opened the little book and read his latest prayer and was shocked at my nine-year-old son's words.

'Did your teacher tell you to write this, Rich?' I asked.

'No, he said we should write a prayer to God about anything that's worrying us.'

The prayer read: 'Dear God, Please help Zimbabwe. All of us don't like what is going on now. So will you please help Zimbabwe and my family and all my friends. Armen.'

Patrick Nabanyama's daughter was arrested briefly by police and interrogated and war veterans swarmed through the centre of Bulawayo. As they had in Chinoyi a couple of months before, the veterans targeted white people and MDC supporters. Three hundred war veterans and government supporters, watched by police, stoned cars, fire-bombed the MDC offices and dragged white people out of their cars and assaulted them. Firemen attempting to extinguish flames engulfing the bombed building were chased away by war veterans and there were numerous street clashes as ordinary people tried to protect themselves as yet another building and car were burnt.

The violence and show of government strength was not restricted to Bulawayo: throughout the country reports came in of war veterans and government supporters parading through the streets demanding vengeance for the murder of Cain Nkala. In my home town I got caught up in the war veterans' show of strength. Crossing the road from the supermarket to my car I heard singing and shouting and the sound of running feet. Nightmares filled my consciousness and I ran to my car to get out of the way of whatever was coming. Sitting behind locked doors and with my heart racing, I had to smile at my own stupidity. A group of perhaps thirty government supporters, escorted by uniformed policemen, came running down the street towards the centre of the little town. They carried placards which said: 'Down with MDC' and 'MDC murderers' and I sat quietly in my car until they and their police escort had gone. They were days of complete madness and the words on everyone's lips were of civil war and martial law, but the days slipped past and gradually things returned to some kind of normalcy.

After the events in Bulawayo, violence in the towns and cities, many of them opposition strongholds, increased to unprecedented levels in the months before the 2002 elections. No one dared speak out for fear of incurring the wrath of war veterans, youths from the Border Gezi training camps, or anyone else claiming to be a government supporter. Being arrested was a real fear for all people, regardless of colour, age and sex, and the paralysed silence intensified to levels unseen before.

NINE

THE MARCH 2002 ELECTIONS – BEFORE AND AFTER

A s the country moved towards the momentous presidential elections, it became increasingly clear that the Zanu PF government was leaving no stone unturned to ensure victory – victory at any cost.

Video footage appeared on Australian television that supposedly showed MDC leader Morgan Tsvangirai discussing with a Canadian company a plot to assassinate President Mugabe. The film was grainy and heavily edited and although it was dismissed worldwide, Zanu PF tried to convince Zimbabwe that it was genuine. Reports came in that Tsvangirai would be charged with treason. Smashing the opposition was uppermost on Zanu PF's election campaign trail and the video provided perfect material for their smear campaign against the MDC.

As well as the massive campaign of violence and intimidation against rural and urban dwellers alike, there was a savage onslaught on individual liberties and human rights. This came in the form of legislation rushed through Parliament in January 2002: the Electoral Act, the Public Order and Security Act and the Access to Information Bill, all designed to drastically curtail any dissenting voices. Even Zanu PF's own legal stalwart, Eddison Zvobgo, strongly condemned the Access to Information Bill. He said 20 of its clauses were unconstitutional and called it 'ill conceived, dangerous' and a 'calculated and determined assault on our liberties'.

South Africa, which had been so quiet for so long, spoke out about the passage of these bills. Archbishop Desmond Tutu, 1984 Nobel Peace Prize winner, said in a BBC interview that Mugabe 'had gone bonkers in a big way' for disregarding the rule of law. Tutu described Zimbabwe as being 'on the slippery slope of perdition'. But while Tutu spoke of eternal death and damnation, South African President Mbeki maintained what had become known as 'quiet diplomacy' and said 'wrong things are happening in our neighbourhood'. The Zimbabwe government was determined and unwavering – it was going for victory in the elections and no one could stop it.

The first of January 2002 was a day like most others, but with it the countdown to the elections began. In 69 days' time we would go to the polls and elect the man who would rule Zimbabwe for the next six years. At last we would know where the future of Zimbabwe lay – and if things would finally begin to get better. Every single Zimbabwean could pin down 26 February 2000 as the date when the madness and mayhem had come out into the open. That was the date when the constitutional referendum had been lost by Zanu PF, the date when farm invasions had started and the date on which all political violence began. It had gone on for almost two years and now, with the presidential elections looming, we wondered if 9 March 2002 would be the day when it would all end. It seemed impossible to believe how low the country had sunk, how much had been destroyed and how many lives had been lost.

Everyone was talking about the elections. The stories of potential rigging were rife and as the ruling party made it harder and harder for the opposition to campaign or for their supporters to walk safely in the streets, we all began to wonder what chance there could be for a free and fair election.

I had an outraged call from friends on a farm just outside Marondera and they told a story that raised the hairs on the back of my neck. At lunchtime on a Sunday, about a month before the elections, one of their workers had gone home to find three strange men pushing his elderly, almost completely blind and diabetic wife into their white car.

'Hey!' he shouted, running towards them. 'Where are you taking my wife?' 'We are taking her to Harare to look after her,' one replied, laughing.

'No,' the man begged. 'I can look after her. Let her go.'

'If you fill in this paper you can have her back,' the men said.

The piece of paper was a ballot slip and the farm worker took it from them.

'You put a cross here,' the men demanded, indicating the space next to Zanu PF on the ballot paper.

The farm worker marked a cross on the ballot paper as ordered. The three men let the woman go and drove away.

Reports like this came in every day and the odds for a free and fair election got lower and lower, but I still could not believe that Zanu PF would win this election. Too many people had lost so much, too many people were unemployed and destitute. The economy was in tatters and inflation was already over 100 per cent.

The government and its supporters had terrorised the nation and kept on doing so right through the last 69 days. Everyone was affected, black and white, men and women, young and old. Farmers and their workers battled to keep going, companies struggled to stay solvent and everyone just wanted it to be over.

The violence and intimidation had got so bad that people began saying that they didn't care any more who won the election. At least after the elections the violence and mayhem would stop, at least we would be able to get on with our lives and make plans for the future, instead of living from hour to hour and day to day. The whole country was on hold: 'after the elections' was the most commonly used phrase in Zimbabwe.

Water pumps in Ruwa broke down and thousands of homes had no water. When asked what was happening, engineers at the Ruwa Rural Council said that they would repair the pumps – after the elections. Telephone lines to dozens of farms around Marondera were out of order and telephone technicians said they would repair the telephones – after the elections. Even in our personal lives we put the most mundane things on hold. Richard needed new shorts for school and I was reluctant to buy them in case the whole country exploded and we had to evacuate. 'But Mum, these ones have got holes,' Richard said to me.

'I promise I'll buy you new ones, Rich – after the elections.'

Richard's shorts went on hold, as did planting of vegetables in my garden, repairs to the roof of my house and almost everything else. In the spare room I had trunks packed with dry and tinned food, piles of blankets and sleeping bags and small suitcases with essential clothes. Documents and precious papers were permanently at the ready and I was one of thousands of people who were ready to evacuate hastily if election results led to violence and mayhem.

The stories of horror kept on pouring in from every corner of the country. A few foreign journalists began to get permits allowing them into the country to cover the elections and knowing there were more people out there reporting on events gave me time to focus on things happening in my own town.

One morning I sat with a Marondera farmer who told me what had happened on his property while he was on leave. In a few days a peaceful, productive and fully operational farm was transformed into a re-education camp. In the months preceding the 2000 parliamentary elections there had been a large number of these centres illegally set up on farms throughout the country. They were back now as the next election loomed and the tactics being used were as crude and disgusting as they had been two years before.

Moments after a farm was vacated, either voluntarily or through coercion, youths, government supporters and shaven-headed men would move in and terrorise the neighbourhood. Using whatever threats they deem suitable, these men demand or simply steal tractors and trailers from nearby farms. As dusk falls the tractors set out in all directions to round up every man, woman and child to be found. People are ordered onto the trailers and then taken to deserted farms for 're-education'. There is no food or water, no one is allowed to rest or leave and groups of people numbering upwards of 400 are re-educated for periods of ten hours or more at a time. They are lectured to about politics, and forced to chant slogans praising the government and condemning the opposition. They are made to raise their arms, with clenched fists, again and again and proclaim undying allegiance to the government. They are forced to line up and run and chant slogans and when they can run no more, they are forced to do press-ups and star jumps. They are made to sing songs popularised during the war for independence and taught new ones that denounce whites, Britain, America, farmers, the MDC and anyone else who is not wholly supportive of the government. Physically exhausted, dirty and hungry, the people are then made to sit in a circle around their 'teachers'.

'Who is the foreman of Farm X?' they are asked.

The foreman of the named farm must stand up and come forward – if he doesn't, people are beaten at random. The foreman stands in front of the instructors. His children are called out of the crowd.

'Beat him,' they are told.

'Hit your father,' they order.

'Hit him harder,' they scream.

Children are forced to kick, beat and whip their own parents. All cultural respect is gone; the father is humiliated, beaten and berated by his own children.

Junior workers from Farm X are called forward. They too are forced to beat the man who is their superior, the man who gives them orders during daylight hours. All job-related respect is gone; workers are forced to beat and humiliate their seniors. When the foreman is broken, physically and mentally, he may crawl back into the crowd. 'Who is the foreman of Farm Y?' the teachers demand. And it starts all over again.

This goes on for most of the night and just before dawn the people are pushed and shoved back onto trailers and taken home. They have been re-educated. They have been humiliated. Dignity and self-respect are gone; they have witnessed at first hand the dangers of free thought and free speech.

By early 2002 there were dozens of empty farms in Mashonaland East, the owners forced off their land and out of their homes. There were dozens of venues where re-education camps operated. On lands where maize should have been a metre tall, with tobacco plants being reaped and paprika bushes flowering, there was just dust. Only dust and marks on the ground from the nights before when people had been re-educated.

In the towns too the re-education and intimidation went on, but the tactics were far more dangerous, as I found out when my own home town became filled with violence inflicted by men who came to do their evil deeds at night. A few streets away from my house a young man who worked in the garden tending flowers and vegetables was called to the gate by a group of men just before dusk. Raymond was accused of being an opposition supporter and taken away through a nearby overgrown swampy area. There he was beaten until he could no longer stand, then held down in the dust while his back was repeatedly cut with a knife. Raymond was branded with a knife and had the letters MDC carved into his back. To stop him from going for help, he was also cut on the tendons at the back of his ankles and stabbed in both buttocks.

Left for dead, Raymond lay where he was for the rest of that night and most of the next day until he gathered enough strength to crawl through the vlei towards his home and safety. He was immediately admitted to a local hospital, where human rights organisations came and took statements and photographs, paid his hospital expenses and left him to recover from the physical terror. Election observers also met with Raymond and heard of his ordeal, documented the facts and expressed their horror and disbelief at the barbaric branding of a human being. Full statements were made to the local police, but nothing was heard in the weeks ahead indicating that the perpetrators had been apprehended. Whilst in hospital Raymond was repeatedly visited by strange men who were government supporters. They did not speak, just stood by his bed for hours at a time. Completely traumatised, but with his physical injuries healing, Raymond was discharged and quietly went home to begin the process of mental recuperation.

On the other side of our little town even a church was taken over by militant government youths, who barricaded the pastor in and accused him of being a supporter of the MDC. Political intervention allowed the pastor to be let out some time later, but the militants stayed behind and used the church as a re-education and torture centre. There were reports of numerous people being taken there and beaten, accused of supporting the opposition. For some time the pastor conducted his Sunday services in the garden of his home, and when he was able to return to his building, he found the walls and floors of the church stained with blood. The youths had also stolen loudspeaker equipment and ripped electrical wiring off the walls. Carpets, chairs, a tape recorder, a tea urn, cups and saucers and children's toys had also been taken by the militants.

In that same week, in the industrial area of the town, a group of 25 government youths arrived outside a large building where the leading members of the opposition were holding their monthly meeting. Many of the bandana-wearing youths were as young as 16. They threw stones, rocks and rubble at the building, smashing all the windows. When the MDC members emerged from the meeting to try and chase the government youths off, there were clashes in the car park and on the street, with people being kicked and beaten in broad daylight. Riot police arrived and did not waste any time, firing rubber bullets at anyone who had not managed to run away in time and arresting everyone who was left.

These were terrifying days: even the most ordinary of outings, such as grocery shopping, were not done without encountering violence and horror. Leaving the supermarket on a Saturday morning with a friend, carrying bags of groceries and with Richard walking at my side, I suddenly heard the sound of shouting and running feet. We turned to see dozens of men running through the main shopping area carrying chunks of wood, table legs and sticks. They, too, were government supporters and had just broken up an opposition meeting at the town's only hotel.

As election day drew closer, carefully selected observers trickled into the country, but most of us knew that this was no more than cheap politicking. For weeks a war had been waging between members of the Zimbabwe government and the world about who would be allowed into the country to observe and monitor the elections. Our foreign affairs and information ministers, and then our President too, said they would only allow foreigners in from some countries to 'observe', but no one would be allowed to 'monitor' the elections except Zimbabweans.

A number of countries were declared 'hostile' and were not allowed in at all; these included Britain, Sweden, Finland, Denmark, Germany and The Netherlands. All of these countries had always been most supportive of Zimbabwe in the 22 years since independence, and indeed during the liberation struggle, pouring billions of dollars into dams, schools, clinics and education projects. For our government now to declare them as 'hostile' was the supreme insult: I felt ashamed to be a Zimbabwean. At every election rally President Mugabe took swipes at the world, and particularly at Britain. He insultingly associated British Prime Minister Tony Blair with the millions of Blair toilets which were all over the country – Blair toilets that had been built and paid for by people in 'hostile' EU countries to improve the health and hygiene of rural people.

Mugabe was adamant that no British people would enter Zimbabwe. He called them 'pink-nosed liars' and would not even allow BBC or Sky reporters and camera crews to cross our borders. A small group of observers from the EU was permitted, as long as it did not include nationals from 'hostile' states. Mostly observers were from other African countries, and the Zimbabwe government started a careful and despicable war of words with the world, insinuating that unless you were black or African you did not have the right or capacity to judge if an African election was free and fair. World leaders, always terrified of criticising black states, for fear of being labelled racists, said nothing. Their silence was a disgrace to world democracy and added fuel to Zanu PF's unstoppable barrage of insults against anyone who dared to criticise. If any of the world's leaders had said anything even remotely insulting about Zimbabwe or her leaders, they would instantly have been called racists and taken to task.

Zanu PF continued to hold all the cards, knowing it was in a win-win situation and would get away with its own reverse racism. Our President and his ministers told the world repeatedly that we were 'a sovereign state' and would not tolerate any interference. When Pierre Schori arrived from Sweden as head of the EU team of observers, our immigration department would only give him a tourist visa – so he, and the entire EU team, left the country. Internal election monitors were all hand-picked by the Zimbabwe government, and the entire electoral process and procedure was completely controlled by Zanu PF, making any chances of a free and fair election about as remote as pigs flying.

Even with some foreign election observers in the country, the violence continued and came frighteningly close to my own door when a neighbour's house was petrol-bombed one evening in mid-February. My dogs had been barking and howling almost continually since a little after dusk and other dogs were barking all over the neighbourhood. The situation in the town, with young militants everywhere, was now so serious that it wasn't safe to go out of the gate at night, and many people would not even venture out of their houses. I tried to quieten my own dogs without much success and neighbours reported hearing glass being broken a little after 8 pm.

About an hour later there was a series of explosions and I ran out of my back door to see a huge fire consuming the house three doors away from mine. A massive orange glow lit the sky, and there were continuing explosions for the next hour as windows and other items in the house heated and exploded. After watching in horror for a few minutes I ran inside to call the police and fire brigade, and for the first time since I had left the farm experienced at first hand the anger and frustration of not being assisted. On the line to the police,

I spoke to a sergeant who gave his name said he could not help because he was unable to make outgoing telephone calls! He said he could not contact the fire brigade and asked me to do so but would not commit himself when I asked again for a police vehicle to be sent round to the site of the burning house.

The next call was to the fire brigade and the man on duty said he too could not help because the fire engine was picking up sick people in a nearby suburb. With my temper rising to explosion level I angrily retorted that I needed a fire engine with water hoses, not an ambulance! The reply was the same, the fire engine is collecting sick people. Imagining groaning people lying amidst hosepipes and ladders, I angrily gave up and knew then without a doubt that this was yet another 'political' issue. Two other people in the neighbourhood made the same calls and got the same responses – and then we put two and two together: the burning house belonged to the opposition MDC candidate and it had been petrol-bombed.

A friend went out into the night and rescued an 80-year-old man who lived immediately next to the burning house and then we sat, helplessly, watching the burning glow lighting up the night. Shortly before 11.00 pm I sat out on my front steps and watched a police vehicle go to what was left of the house. It did not stop, just hooted two or three times and left. For the next hour there was whistling from all directions as the men in the night regrouped and left.

The morning after the petrol-bombing the neighbourhood was full of strange youths and men, many wearing overalls and large hats, who stood on corners, lolled against street lamps or sat on kerbs. No one dared go anywhere near the gutted building, and this in itself was proof that it had been a political statement. Later in the morning I spoke to the owner of the house and was horrified to hear that an adult and two children had been there at the time of the attack. Men had come and broken windows, entered the house and stolen a radio, TV, camera, video, bicycle and clothing. They had then left, throwing petrol bombs into the bedroom wing of the house. One-third of the house was completely destroyed, all the windows broken, and the roofing timbers consumed. The asbestos roof had collapsed and shattered into small pieces. One child had hidden under a bed at the other end of the house; the other child and the adult managed to escape after the looters had left and while the house was on fire they hid in the garden. The children were rescued and evacuated to Harare in the early hours of the morning and were safe but extremely traumatised.

By mid-morning on the day following the petrol-bombing, the owner had still been unable to get an official from the fire brigade to go to his gutted house – not even to inspect the ashes for forensic evidence. In the days that followed there were a number of people arrested: not the perpetrators of the act, but the man who had rescued the children in the early hours and the men who had been round to take photographs of the gutted building. Also arrested were two security guards whom the house owner employed to look after the remains of his life. This was clear warning to us all not to be seen helping and not to get involved. This example was just one of scores happening all over the country; elections could not come soon enough.

Election day finally arrived and I left home shortly after six in the morning on the first day, prepared for a long wait. The lists of polling stations had only been announced two days before and the number of urban ballot centres had been slashed across the country by almost 40 per cent. In Marondera town polling stations had been reduced in number from eleven to four, and I knew the queues would be long but was absolutely determined to vote regardless of how long I had to wait. I was number 152 in line, but didn't really think that would be a problem because when the doors opened at 7.00 am I assumed the queue would move at a fair speed.

The mood all around me was easy, jovial and friendly. Everyone had determination written all over their faces and jokes flew fast and furious. I couldn't remember when I'd last heard so much laughter or felt so happy, welcome and at ease in my own country. Black and white people stood together, joked together and shared sandwiches and drinks. It was a bitterly cold and misty morning and hands and feet turned to icy blocks as the hours passed and the line moved hardly at all.

I had no idea if I would be allowed to vote when I got to the front of the line. So many of my friends had had their names struck off the register because their parents had not been born in Zimbabwe. My parents were not born here either, but I was, and I was determined to try and vote. After four hours and ten minutes I got to the front of the line, shocked that fewer than 40 people an hour were voting. By now there were perhaps 5 000 people behind me and I knew that they would not all get to the front of the line before the station closed. My hands, though frozen, were clammy with sweat as the official turned the printed pages on the roll looking for my name amongst the ba's and be's. I found my own name, he smiled at me and with a feeling of absolute elation I put a cross on a small piece of paper, with huge pride and satisfaction. My fingers were sticky with the yellow dye that would prevent me from voting again and that stuck to the steering wheel of my car as I drove home humming.

The phone rang incessantly throughout the day and the stories were the same from everywhere. The queues were enormous, the mood was ecstatic, the determination was phenomenal. Great flasks of coffee and soup and mountains of sandwiches were made and delivered to election monitors, and for me this was the most wonderful day of the past two years. Friends in Harare waited six, eleven, even 13 hours to vote. Many did not vote that first day, but were still determined to go back and try again on the second and final day.

Thousands of people never got to the front of those voting queues. Thousands more did, only to find that their names had been struck off the registers for a host of reasons – or for no reason at all. Reports flooded in of irregularities and 1 400 people, many of them polling agents, were arrested and charged with all sorts of things the police said were offences, including giving out information on where polling stations were located, handing out sandwiches and carrying walkie-talkie radios. The mood again darkened as we heard of ballot boxes disappearing, of numbers not matching, of box bottoms falling out, of war veterans sitting inside polling stations, of villagers being forced to stand in line behind their headmen. The results were going to be announced constituency by constituency, and war veterans, militants and government supporters would know which constituencies had voted for which man. An emergency court ruling extended voting to a third day in Harare, but polling stations did not open until 11.00 am and the confusion was supreme.

The results were announced live on ZBC television and, as I had done in 2000, I sat up all night with paper, pencil and calculator. The Registrar General, Tobaiwa Mudede, announced the results painfully slowly, first in Shona, then in Ndebele, and finally in English. Since English is Zimbabwe's official language, this was ridiculous. After a few hours Mudede spoke only English and stopped using people's first and middle names. The figures coming in did not make any sense at all. Constituencies that had always been solidly MDC were suddenly Zanu PF. Outlying, remote rural villages suddenly had thousands more votes than previously registered voters, and suspicion mounted when Mudede went quiet for over five hours when the last tallies were still to be announced. By midday the final figures were announced, and Robert Mugabe was again the President of Zimbabwe. The opposition immediately declared that it would not accept the results. The army was put on high alert around the country and armed police were thick on the ground in towns and cities.

Within days foreign election observers began producing their reports, condemning the results and declaring that the elections had been neither free nor fair. The head of the Norwegian observer team said: 'There is no way these elections can be described as substantially free and fair.' The US Secretary of State, Colin Powell, said: 'Mr Mugabe may claim victory but not democratic legitimacy' and the US Secretary of State for African Affairs, Walter Kansteiner, was even more outspoken. 'The independent media was persecuted, civil society was marginalised and the will of the people was the chief casualty.' The Nigerian head of the 42 Commonwealth observers also condemned the elections and talked of a 'systematic campaign of intimidation' in which thousands of people had been disenfranchised. Zimbabwe held its breath waiting to see what South Africa would say, knowing that this report would be the most critical in deciding events in the days ahead.

Overseeing the 50-strong team of South African observers was Sam Motsuenyane, who must have felt more than a little uncomfortable as he sat in front of journalists in Harare. Less than a fortnight before the elections two South African observers had had their car stoned by government supporters in Kwekwe. A convoy of SADC observers, in clearly marked vehicles, had also been attacked by government youths in Chinoyi. Five vehicles had their windows shattered by stone-throwing government youths and three Botswana observers were injured in the attack. Duke Lefhoko, leader of the South African team of observers, had condemned the campaign as being not free and said the country was 'in a state of fear'. He said: 'We have seen the police in action with our own eyes and they are unresponsive, uncooperative and won't talk to people.' With this evidence and these statements, Sam Motsuenyane would surely have to agree with what everyone else was saying, but he did not. The South African businessman announced that Zimbabwe's elections had been 'legitimate'. Mr Motsuenyane was jeered and laughed at by assembled journalists, and diplomats walked out of the press conference.

The country descended into a deep, dark hole of disbelief and depression. We felt betrayed by our nearest neighbours. Again Archbishop Desmond Tutu spoke out in the strongest terms. 'I am deeply, deeply, deeply distressed that our country could be among those who say the election was legitimate or free and fair when we are claiming to be adherents to democracy.' Archbishop Tutu's distress mirrored our own; we were disgusted. President Mbeki said very little, but he and the Nigerian and Australian presidents met as a Commonwealth Troika. In a four-hour meeting the three leaders agreed that Zimbabwe should immediately be suspended from the Council of the Commonwealth.

Zimbabwe's propaganda merchants immediately trashed the Commonwealth and said the suspension meant nothing. They tried very hard to make us believe that the decision had been a racist one, but there was no disguising the fact that this was a huge blow to President Mugabe and Zanu PF, whose Nigerian and South African brothers had broken ranks for the first time. The EU imposed targeted sanctions on President Mugabe and 19 other top officials, including ministers, army chiefs and police commanders. The sanctions included an arms embargo, a travel ban on the 20 named officials and the freezing of their assets abroad. Days later America imposed similar sanctions, Switzerland announced that it would freeze relevant bank accounts and Denmark announced that its Harare embassy was closing down.

Victory for Zanu PF, whether by fair means or foul, may have been sweet but they again had the mandate to run a country that was in the most diabolical mess. We stood as a country almost completely on our own, cut off and condemned by donors, banks and governments across the globe. Hunger, unemployment, inflation and economic collapse were still a part of Zimbabwe under Robert Mugabe, as were the endlessly long queues for milk, maize meal, sugar and cooking oil. Victory for Zanu PF came back to haunt us at every turn and Zimbabwe descended into political violence and retribution in every part of the country.

The retribution did not come from the losers of the election but from the winners, who flaunted their arrogance and flexed their muscles. Thousands more people were beaten, tortured and chased away from their homes and villages. Hundreds of people who had helped in the elections were hunted down and went into hiding; hundreds of others were attacked for little or no reason. Many more people were murdered, and anyone even remotely suspected of having helped the MDC became a victim at the hands of government supporters. I met one such man in our local hospital after he had been brutally assaulted by men wielding pick handles.

Less than a week after the elections, Jon Jon, a young farm manager, was ordered by war veterans and government youths to go to his farm workers' village. When he arrived there he was accused of having given a cell phone to an MDC polling agent. Lying in the dirt was one of his employees, Darlington, a security guard on the farm. Darlington had been beaten continuously and was clearly dying. As men started interrogating Jon Jon, he soon found that it didn't matter what answer he gave, they were still going to beat him. They took turns to hit him on his backside with wooden pick handles.

Darlington tried to intervene. 'My boss didn't do anything,' he cried as the men lashed into Jon Jon who lay sprawled face down in the dust.

Jon Jon pleaded again and again for them to stop, saying that Darlington needed to get to hospital, that the man was dying. Finally the attackers ordered Jon Jon to take Darlington to hospital, but it was too late, and by the time Jon Jon arrived in Marondera, Darlington was already dead. Jon Jon drove himself to another hospital and it was there I met him the following evening.

The room was full of people, mostly men, laughing and drinking beer out of tins and smoking.

'Hi, Cathy – do you want to see my arse!' Jon Jon said, moments after I'd been introduced. Before I could say a word and with shouts of laughter from all the visitors in the room, Jon Jon lifted the sheet that lay lightly over him. There was massive purple and almost black bruising all over his buttocks and right up between his legs and around his groin. It was absolutely horrific: all I could compare it to was dye – as if someone had spilled gentian violet and black paint all over him.

I did not know what to say or how to react: Jon Jon's words and action were the last thing I had expected. There was a lot more laughing and joking and it took me a while to realise that this was Jon Jon's way of coping. It was delayed shock, I suppose: if you didn't laugh you would cry – just sob and sob. We all stood around and drank beers and smoked for a while and at one point I went out of the room to talk to one of the nurses. She asked if we could please stay as long as possible, because more than anything Jon Jon needed to be normal, needed to feel safe and loved by his friends. Gradually people left, and almost as soon as they had gone Jon Jon asked me to come and sit close to the bed. We talked then for over an hour and he just wanted to tell me everything again and again. I knew this feeling so well, almost as if the terror has been so horrific that you just have to keep talking about it in order to keep sane.

Jon Jon, now that his friends had gone, was very emotional and his story was disjointed. It seemed as if the beatings had gone on for quite some time and been done by different people. They would question him for a while and then beat him. At some point Jon Jon's wife had gone to the workers' village and the attackers had started on her as well. One minute they were taunting her and pulling her hair and then the next they would ask her about her baby. Did she have teeth yet, was she eating porridge yet? One of the people supervising the interrogation and beating was a woman, and apparently she was ruthless and completely without mercy. As Jon Jon talked he cried and held my hand, sometimes so tightly that my fingers were numb, but at least for him the nightmare was over. For thousands of others it was just beginning, as mobs of men moved around the farming areas and began evicting people from their homes.

When I met some of these families I was horrified at what was happening to them and within a few days it all became frighteningly real for me too as the tenants on Stow Farm were evicted with two hours' notice and everything I had been trying so hard to forget for two years became cold, ugly reality again.

TEN

FULL CIRCLE

A month before the 2002 elections the tenants leasing Stow Farm phoned to tell me that there had been a new invasion of the property. For almost sixteen months the farm had been relatively peaceful. War veterans squatting there had left shortly after my family moved out and the tenants had been left alone. Now the war veterans were back to muster support for the government as the elections got closer. They were not the same men who had been there in 2000, but they used the same tactics. A tent was erected in the field below the house, the fence was cut, dozens of trees were axed, a latrine was dug and then they began their own election campaign. They held weekly and then daily meetings in the field, made demands for food and ordered people in the neighbourhood to come to their meetings and swear allegiance to Zanu PF. Their numbers increased at night and chanting, drumming and singing could be heard from the farmhouse. The tenants on the farm made reports to the police, but nothing was done and the invaders were left undisturbed.

It was soon discovered that more than just political meetings were being held in the fields. The dozen or so men living in the tent would bring MDC supporters there at night and beat them. Six teenage boys caught waving to girls were accused of having waved with an open palm – of secretly signalling their support for the MDC. The six were taken to the tent on Stow Farm at night, ordered to strip and lie down on the ground and were then whipped severely with branches and sticks. Their wounds were appalling: reports were made to both election observers and human rights organisations, but there was nothing anyone could do about it.

I was sickened to think of the blood on the fields where once we had grazed our sheep and cattle, where Richard had run happy and carefree on his adventures with his friends. As we had in 2000, we hoped and prayed that after the elections all these men would have to pay the price of their evil deeds.

On 1 March 2002, exactly two years to the day since Stow Farm had originally been invaded by war veterans, the property was listed for Compulsory Acquisition by the Government of Zimbabwe. I sat in my car outside a small Marondera shop and cried when I read the notice in the *Herald* newspaper.

> Land Acquisition Act. (Chapter 20:10)
> Preliminary notice to Compulsorily Acquire Land.
> LOT 39.
> Notice is hereby given in terms of subsection (1) of section 5 of the Land Acquisition Act (Chapter 20:10) that the President intends to acquire compulsorily the land described in the Schedule for resettlement ... purposes. A plan of the land is available for inspection at the following offices of the Ministry of Lands, Agriculture and Rural Resettlement ...
> Any owner or occupier or any other person who has an interest and right in the said land, and who wishes to object to the proposed compulsory acquisition, may lodge the same in writing, with the Minister of Lands, Agriculture and Rural Resettlement on or before the 1st of April 2002.
> J.M. Made.
> Minister of Lands, Agriculture and Rural Resettlement.
> 65. Deed of transfer 4582/91 registered in the name of Samanga Cash Store P/L, in respect of certain piece of land situate in the district of Marandellas, being Stow Estate, measuring three hundred and ninety four comma seven five (394,75) hectares.

For two years I had been expecting this very day, this exact notice – and here it was, in ugly black and white for everyone to see. By March 2002 over 95 per cent of commercial farms had been listed for compulsory acquisition. I had no idea why mine was one of the last to be listed. Perhaps the authorities had finally caught up with me, finally realised that I was the annoying woman who kept writing letters to the world and articles to newspapers. More likely, though, was the fact that I had just slipped their notice – but now the day had come.

There were two errors in the notice that should have rendered it worthless in law, but I wasn't holding my breath. I immediately phoned the tenants leasing Stow Farm, as it was to them the official government papers would most probably be served. By law, if any laws were going to be followed, a Section 5 Notice of Intention to Compulsorily Acquire had to be served within 30 days of the notice appearing in the newspaper. I lodged an official objection to the Preliminary Notice in the *Herald* and then the days of March passed. The elections came and went but no Section 5 Notice was served. In late March the men camping in the tent on the fields of Stow Farm left as suddenly as they had come. When April arrived and still no official papers had come, the acquisition notice was rendered null and void according to Zimbabwe's own laws.

A strange and uneasy quiet descended on the farm. The tenants carried on as normal and we just waited for the next move from the Minister of Lands, war veterans or anyone in officialdom. We didn't have long to wait. The week of Zimbabwe's 22nd anniversary of independence arrived and all over the country groups of men went from farm to farm demanding food, money and transport so that they could celebrate independence. They arrived at Stow Farm and ordered the tenants to give them a cow. This demand was refused, as there were only dairy cows on the farm, so the men at the gate settled for milk instead. Three days later they decided that a few litres of milk a day was not enough.

Once again a mob arrived at the gate of Stow Farm. This time their demands were more serious. They ordered the tenants and farm workers to vacate the property and houses within two days. There was no negotiating with the men; they had made their minds up that now Stow Farm belonged to them completely. They were threatening, abusive and frightening. The police were immediately contacted but they said that until there was theft or violence they could do nothing, as it was a 'political' matter. These were nightmare days, with the tenants, their three children, all the workers and their families packing as fast as they could – throwing things into boxes without even knowing where they were going, just that they had to get out, praying that they would do so unhurt.

I knew there was nothing I could do to help my tenants, who had family and friends helping them, and that I would be of far more use to my neighbours over the road from Stow Farm, who had been given a similar eviction demand. They were a couple in their seventies, who had no family to help them and had been in their house for 23 years. Their little farm of only 300 acres had never been invaded or squatted on; they had not been listed for government seizure, and the eviction came completely out of the blue with no warning of impending trouble.

Arriving at Micky and Myrtle's farm late on Saturday afternoon with a friend to help, I got out of the car and embraced Micky. This elderly man who had taught me everything I knew about farming and who had become such a dear friend over the years wept as I put my arms around him. They had lost their farm in Kenya at the time of the Mau Mau, they had lost their farm in Inyanga during the independence war, and now it was all happening again

Myrtle too wept when we embraced and I could hardly credit the magnitude of their anguish and the size of the task at hand. With only one day left to complete the job of getting out of their home of 23 years, the task was mammoth. Cupboards and drawers had to be emptied, sorted and packed. Pictures had to be taken off walls, curtains unhooked from rails and books removed from shelves. Carpets had to be rolled up and furniture pushed into one room ready for the seven-ton truck that would arrive at eight the following morning. I had come with cardboard boxes, newspapers and Sellotape and Myrtle simply pointed to one of numerous piles and told me what to pack and what to leave.

I could see the multitude of emotions consuming Myrtle – anger, regret and even bitterness. We just worked as fast as we could. It was dark when we heard a car hoot at the gate. It was the vet. He had come to give the dogs an overdose of anaesthetic. We sat together in the small living room and had a strong drink. This was the moment they had been dreading the most – putting the dogs to sleep because there would be no room for them at the tiny cottage they had managed to find in the town. The dogs were fat, sleek, happy farm dogs and the kindest thing was to put them to sleep. I tried to chatter to take their minds off what was going on outside the room, but my words became a sort of senseless gabble and in the end we just sat with our drinks, each no doubt remembering all the times that had gone before.

After I had left Micky and Myrtle for the night I could hardly bear the agony of what was happening to them, to their lives and to the whole neighbourhood. It was all so senseless and destructive: so many innocent lives, both human and animal, were being destroyed by a few power-hungry people.

On the day of Micky and Myrtle's ordered eviction from their home, I arrived at the farm a little after seven in the morning. Already the war veterans were there. I felt both scared and angry as I drove down their familiar driveway and saw these vultures waiting and patrolling. I did not want to be here or ever to feel like this again: the temptation to do a U-turn and just get out of there as fast as I could was great. The man in charge, who called himself Wind, stepped out into the driveway in front of my car. He wore one-piece orange overalls, a brown belt at his waist and a large hat. Sticking out of his back pocket on a thin pole was a Zimbabwean flag, and at his side trotted a scrawny little black and yellow dog with wild eyes. There were half a dozen other men hanging around and they lolled against fence- and gate-posts with arrogant, defiant looks on their faces. Determined that I would neither stop nor speak to these men, I looked straight ahead. I did not make eye contact but drove around Wind and his dog towards the gate, which was being held open for me.

The chaos in the house was supreme. Every surface was covered with boxes and cartons. Every room had piles of things in corners which were to be left behind and there seemed no end to the chaos. This was not a home anymore, the memories had gone, the happy times would be no more, it was just a dirty, echoing building and when the truck arrived it came almost with a sense of relief. Throughout the few hours it took us to pack and load, Wind and his men stood at the gateway. They would not let us load or take any of the farm equipment because this, according to the recent pronouncements of the Agriculture Minister, now belonged to the farm.

We left behind everything, including a tractor and plough, grain bins, drums of fuel, lawnmowers, wheelbarrows, feed tins, 190 laying chickens and hundreds of common agricultural tools. Other farmers trying to take their equipment had been stopped by war veterans, had things confiscated and even trashed. There was no point in taking any chances; we all wanted to get out of there without incident, and so Micky and Myrtle left behind the very fabric of their 50 years in farming. Like thieves Myrtle and I raced out to her vegetable garden with baskets and bags and hurriedly dug out a few potatoes and carrots. There was no time to cut down hands of bananas or pluck nearly ripe pawpaws from the trees in her garden. Wind was getting restless, eviction time had arrived and he wanted us out. A couple of youths climbed a tree near the gate and watched our every move, occasionally calling out something, but we tried to ignore them.

When finally the truck was full and the doors closed Micky and Myrtle walked from room to room. There were no words, nothing anyone could say that would comfort them or make any of this all right. There was only one word I could think of to describe this utter hell and, once again, that word was ... obscene. It was utterly obscene that a few arbitrary men at the gate had the power to do this and that the police would not intervene. It was Zimbabwe's dirty politics that had encouraged and allowed this to happen and the world needed to hear this shameful story.

Almost as soon as Micky and Myrtle had left their farm and home, Wind and his men took the keys and installed themselves firmly as the new owners. The situation was exactly the same on Stow Farm – the tenants left and the war veterans moved into the house. Wind and a handful of men had now taken over both farms and all the buildings. Five days after they had moved into what used to be my family's home they sent a message to me. The borehole was broken and I should come and fix it. This one ridiculous message incensed me and I responded with an unrepeatable two-word answer. I then attempted to see the District Administrator in the town to explain the situation on Stow Farm, to tell him that unknown men had evicted all the people from their homes on the farm, had moved into the main house, taken over the trading store – and the police would do nothing about it.

I did eventually get to see the DA, and the meeting was not pleasant. This senior government official was not alone; all his meetings were held with a member of the CIO present, and I felt distinctly uncomfortable at having to tell of my personal anguish in front of this second man who lolled casually in a chair. Calmly and politely I told the DA that I now held the government of Zimbabwe responsible for securing the assets – both fixed and movable – that remained on Stow Farm. I had already written a letter to the DA, PA, Governor, Minister of Agriculture and Member in Charge of Police stating the events and including a list that ran to two pages of the assets on Stow Farm. I had not received a response to the letter and now attempted to state the same facts calmly to the DA.

For the first five minutes he listened calmly to what I had to say. He announced that the eviction of the tenants was not allowed, and, while I sat in front of him, he phoned the District Police and briefed them on the situation. I explained to the DA that I was very worried that the men now living in the house would strip the assets – and aside from losing the farm, the infrastructure would also be lost. I explained that since no official government acquisition papers had been served on me and since the police would not help me, I was at a loss as to what to do or who to turn to for assistance. What had been a quiet and polite discussion suddenly turned into a frightening tirade.

'Do you or your tenants want to go back to Stow Farm?' he asked. 'No!' I answered. 'How can we go back there when strange men are frightening us and threatening us and the police will not come to our assistance?'

'You people!' he suddenly shouted, leaning across the desk and pointing his finger at me. 'You people. You have demonised President Mugabe. You have demonised Zimbabwe. You have sent all your papers and letters and lies to the world and then you come crying for help. You people! You should go back to Britain. Do you want to go back on your farm?'

'No, not under these circumstances,' I answered quietly, feeling both scared and threatened in the office of this government official.

'Good!' he said, rubbing his small hands together, 'very good, this is exactly what we want. It is better this way!'

'I just want to secure the assets and make sure they are not being stripped and sold,' I said, and that statement led to another outburst.

'We will secure everything,' he shouted. 'You just go to the Ministry of Lands, give them the Title Deeds and then we will value everything.'

I tried to leave, but the man was not finished with his lecture and I sat quietly in front of him being admonished like a child by a headmaster. When at last he paused to draw breath I stood up and thanked him for his time. As I left the building and walked to my car, the Marondera District Administrator and his CIO minder stood at the window and watched me. It took a lot of effort for me to hold my head up and walk tall. Almost the last ounce of pride and dignity had been taken from me.

There was nothing more I could do: in that same week 19 other farmers in Marondera and 250 in other parts of the country were similarly evicted from their homes and farms by arbitrary men who called themselves war veterans. In a sickening example of government hypocrisy, less than one week later the same DA who had berated and belittled me toured farms in the district, telling all farmers still in their homes that they must be patriotic and plant wheat.

This DA, and others all over the country, told the farmers they would be left in peace to grow their wheat – but aside from their word there were no other guarantees. No guarantees that the farmer's crop wouldn't suddenly be taken over by war veterans or militants; no guarantee that the state wouldn't come and seize the wheat at harvest time as it had done with maize; no guarantee that the farmer wouldn't be thrown out of his house before the crop had been harvested. Farmers who had eviction notices, whose land was squatted, whose workers had been beaten, who were no longer allowed to sell or take their own equipment off their farms – were now expected to be patriotic and grow another crop.

Sitting quietly in my Marondera house a few days later, reading *Schindler's Ark*, I was struck by the terrifying similarities between Nazi Germany in 1940 and Zimbabwe in 2002. The author, Thomas Keneally, describes the first street slaughter of Jews in the ghetto and says: 'Beyond this day no thinking person could fail to see what would happen.' After the widespread evictions of farmers from their homes in Zimbabwe and after my meeting with the DA, I knew there would be no turning back. Too many people had endured too much. They would never go back to their farms. They would not ever want to return to those places which had so many memories – both good and bad. Beyond this point there would inevitably be years of hunger and poverty in Zimbabwe. If three men had managed in only five days to burn out a borehole motor on Stow Farm, how long would it take for tractors, computerised irrigation equipment and other highly specialised infrastructure to be similarly destroyed?

A few days later another message came to me from Stow Farm. The little trading store which had been so lovingly kept and tended by Jane had been re-opened by Wind and his colleagues. The shelves were not stocked with bread and buns or biscuits and sugar any more. There were no more fresh and boiled eggs or baby porridge and washing powder. There were no bowls of tomatoes and plums or bundles of rape and spinach. The store now sold only two things, Chibuku beer and popcorn. As a country we had slipped back too far; too many decades of work and development had been destroyed and commandeered by men who were not farmers but merely government pawns and people out to make as much money as they could.

By the end of May 2002 I did not know if I still belonged or was wanted in the country of my birth. I knew that the madness could not go on much longer and that the economy had almost completely collapsed. As each farmer was chased out and as every business closed down the loss to the country was enormous – in skills, expertise, taxes and revenue. Zimbabwe stood as a fragmented nation with divisions at every level. Marriages had broken up, families had been separated, communities divided. There was not a lot of hope on the horizon, but there were still too many good and brave people standing up for themselves and their country to give up.

There was Short Wave Radio Africa, which for three hours every night told us the truth about what was happening in Zimbabwe. There were the brave journalists of the *Daily News, Zimbabwe Independent* and *Financial Gazette* who were being arrested almost daily but who still did not stop telling us what was really going on. There were all the supporters and members of the MDC who were still beaten and arrested, intimidated and on the run. There were people on the other side of the world compiling a daily e-mail report called ZW News, with a readership of millions. There were thousands of people outside Zimbabwe helping to spread the word, building web sites, putting together information bulletins, raising money and donating food, medicines and clothing. There were thousands more lobbying their MPs, senators and governments to help Zimbabwe.

Most days those of us in the thick of it in Zimbabwe felt as if we were alone, but we were not. Often it was hard to see the wood for the trees as this evil political game was played out, but we would not give up. The suffering of millions of Zimbabweans must not have been in vain.

The much-talked-about dialogue between the MDC and Zanu PF immediately following the elections in March 2002 collapsed before it even started, postponed indefinitely by Zanu PF. The New Partnership for Africa's Development (NEPAD) hung in the balance now. NEPAD talked about international donor governments giving US$64 billion annually to Africa, but its foundation stone was a commitment by African leaders to uphold global standards of democracy and good governance. Perhaps it was the tantalising taste of billions of American dollars that had made African leaders turn a blind eye to two years of state-sponsored terror in Zimbabwe. The World Food Programme had already begun feeding seven million starving people in Zimbabwe, once the breadbasket of Africa, but regional leaders said nothing about the man and the government in power for 22 years or their policy of systematically preventing farmers from growing food. They said nothing about 160 people murdered, thousands tortured and raped and 100 000 internal refugees. Regional African leaders who continued to praise Mugabe's policies of giving land back to landless people held out their hands for US$64 billion and said nothing as the lists were published of the new owners of Zimbabwe's farms.

In the first fortnight of May 2002, the Zimbabwe government said it had begun evicting settlers squatting on commercial farms. Agriculture Minister Joseph Made said the eviction of settlers was being done so that 'systematic land resettlement' could take place. Home Affairs Minister John Nkomo referred to the 12 000 people being evicted in one province as 'pretenders and impostors' who should go back to where they had come from. He said the eviction exercise would take place countrywide. The Minister said settlers being evicted would be given land somewhere else at a later date. Settlers who had voted for Zanu PF on the promise of land were now, just two months after the election, being evicted. That same promise of being given land elsewhere had been made to white farmers by President Mugabe in 2000, but had also not been kept. Black and white alike, we were all just pawns in a nation that thrived on broken promises.

Zimbabwe appeared to have come full circle – but, as always in our country, nothing was ever as it seemed. The names of the new owners of Zimbabwe's grabbed farms were published in the *Financial Gazette* on Thursday, 23 May 2002. The names were not of graduates from farming colleges and institutions, they were of those who had toed the party line and done the dirty work. The list of Zimbabwe's new commercial farmers was a Who's Who in Zanu PF.

It included:
Chief Justice Godfrey Chidyausiku
Vice President Joseph Msika
Deputy President Simon Muzenda
Security Minister Nicholas Goche
Army Commander Constantine Chiwenga
Prison Director Paradzayi Zimondi
President Mugabe's sister Sabina Mugabe
President Mugabe's brother-in-law Reward Marufu
Police Commissioner Augustine Chihuri.

Other named beneficiaries included cabinet ministers and their wives and relations, governors, senior army and police personnel, permanent secretaries, diplomats and even correspondents in the ZBC. Zanu PF had promised land to the people – but which people? In May 2002 white farmers and black settlers were both the same – impostors on Zanu PF's land.

ELEVEN

POSTSCRIPT

Two weeks after I had finished writing this book and when the manuscript had been submitted to the publishers, I received a phone call from the last farmer left in the neighbourhood of Stow Farm. He told me that hundreds of people were being dumped by government officials on our farm and that he feared a major humanitarian crisis was looming. Even though I had promised myself that I would never return to Stow Farm and that I did not want to see what was going on, I couldn't help myself from going back one last time.

I was scared as I got into the passenger seat of a friend's car. Scared of the men who had taken over the farmhouse, scared of getting involved in a confrontation and scared of the memories. On my lap I had a notebook, in my pocket was my ID and in my hand a cell phone. Aside from that, my friend and I carried nothing; the less we had with us, the less there was that could be taken away from us if we were stopped or mobbed. I didn't want to talk as we drove, I just sat with my hands on my lap, knuckles white from being clenched. I could feel my own fingernails biting into the palms of my hands and that helped me to keep focused.

As we drove along the narrow tar road, everything was so familiar and yet so different. On a big timber plantation of a farm long since evacuated, hundreds of trees had gone, felled for the fires of the new occupants. Kilometres of farm fencing had completely disappeared, as had road signs and farm name boards; everywhere there was the look of neglect. On the edges of the road the soft sand was thick and had banked up into perilous piles and on the verges the last of the cosmos flowers blossomed in glorious shades of pink and purple. Two vervet monkeys scampered across the road in front of us and eased themselves up into a Munondo tree, its crown blanketed with velvety brown pods. For a moment I tried to concentrate my attention on that one very familiar sight, clinging to the sanity of its normalcy.

We were nearing Stow Farm and I couldn't decide if I wanted my friend to slow down or speed up; my hands had gone clammy and my breathing was fast – and yet I felt so very cold. I wanted to just squeeze my eyes closed and not see what was coming up around the next bend, but I could not and just stared in horror as we drove slowly along the boundary fence of Stow Farm. The fields were filled with tall brown grass but were deserted of both animals and people. Many of the trees that had always been landmarks were gone or showed signs of being stripped of their wood. The huge lucky bean tree in the top field that should have been covered with crimson winter flowers had most of its branches missing, hacked off for firewood. My eyes burned with tears as I remembered how many hundreds of times I had sat under that tree or collected the little black and red seeds with Richard.

'Slow down, please slow down,' I whispered anxiously to my friend as I shoved a baseball cap onto my head, attempting anonymity, and we passed the two men who were undoubtedly the war veterans guarding the premises. The men wore dirty blue overalls and floppy bush hats and sat on the verge outside the gate, staring arrogantly as we crawled past, perhaps daring us to stop or turn in at the signboard which still proclaimed that this was Stow Farm.

I stared in shock at the sight of what had been our peaceful tree-lined driveway. I could see people everywhere. Men were gathering firewood in what was left of the gum plantation, women were hanging washing on the fence lines and children were running in and out of the paddocks in the dairy. There was washing everywhere; on fence lines and posts, hanging on gates and draped over shrubs and bushes. The entire length of the driveway was lined with houses. They were little square buildings of sticks and branches covered with old and tattered plastic. Some of the shacks were made of rusted sheets of tin leaning against one another, tied together with raffia, wire and strips of bark. Slowly we drove past and could see many more shacks between the gum trees. A few white goats wandered aimlessly amongst what had become a compact squatter camp.

The shock was beginning to sink in and I tried hard to bury all the memories that those trees held for me. How I had driven to a co-operative nursery in Dema and collected every single seedling, loading them into my truck with Richard handing them to me one by one. How Richard and I, with the help of only two workers, had dug holes and planted every single one of the 800 trees. How we had, me with secateurs and Richard with scissors, carefully trimmed the side shoots to encourage the trees to grow straight. I tried not to think about how it had always been a place of such peace and solitude for me. How I had wandered beneath the trees, picking crimson flame lilies at Christmas time. How we had carved Richard's name into the bark of one of the trees and how often we had stood watching as hundreds of Abdim's Storks roosted in the branches throughout the rainy season. There were so many happy and peaceful memories that had been replaced with a sea of ugly shacks.

At the farm store that had been turned into a beerhall, there were only men to be seen – sitting drinking on the veranda, leaning against the walls and spilling out onto the roadway. Gone forever was the sight of Jane, sitting on an upturned crate in the sun, knitting endless pairs of green gloves while she waited for customers. In what had been the farm workers' village there were still more people, and for just a moment a decade of images flashed through my mind. I could see Richard playing in the dust with the workers' children, could hear their squeals of glee as they had races with home-made wire cars whose wheels were made of polish tin lids. I could hear the sweet piping voice of two-year-old Cecilia calling out to me as she had so many hundreds of times when I had passed on my way to the store. I could see her tiny hands held out for the toffee I almost always had for her in my pocket, could hear the little muffled popping sound her cupped hands made as they clapped their thanks.

Nothing and no one was familiar here now; all the people were strangers, and we drove on. In the field where the borehole was, the pump house and security cage protecting the precious water point had been demolished and the materials were gone. The little field around the borehole was a sea of weeds, snake apple, blackjacks and khaki bush. Gone was the lush and life-saving Kikuyu grass that had sustained all our sheep and their lambs throughout winter. It was to this field, so close to the house, that we had gone with bottles of milk to feed orphaned lambs, and where I had spent so many hours docking lambs' tails and testicles and putting yellow number tags into their ears. Now there was nothing to see except neglect and destruction.

At the nearby tobacco barns there were more strange people with their washing draped on every possible surface. I wondered if the Spotted Eagle Owl still lived there, still raised her chicks in the nest high up in the gum tree that stood sentinel next to the building. We drove slowly down the main road and away from the home complex, along the boundary fence of the farm. There were a few women walking towards the little dam and a couple of men sitting on the ground in a field where a herd of perhaps 20 thin black cattle grazed in the dry grass. We went right down the length of the boundary fence and I was sure I would see squatters' huts everywhere, but there was nothing to see. The farm itself was completely deserted. There was no sign of any sort of production whatsoever, no crops were being grown, not even small vegetable patches.

I am not ashamed to say that I did not go into Stow Farm. I had seen enough but I had also been seen. For ten years I had lived with my family on that corner farm and there were not many people who did not know who I was. Returning to my warm and safe house in Marondera I sank into a deep depression which almost engulfed me, but the phone kept on ringing and I had many calls and visits from people who had seen me looking at the ruination of Stow Farm. People who lived in the area were desperate to tell me exactly what had been happening on the farm since the tenants had been evicted six weeks before, and their eyewitness accounts were far more shocking than the little I had been able to see.

All my conversations were with the black people whom I had always done business with on the farm. For so long, these same people had not felt able to talk to me. Just as I had found when writing the stories in this book, the vast majority of ordinary black Zimbabweans did not want to tell their stories. Those who did talk to me always asked that I did not use their names or identify their villages and home areas. They did not want people to know what had happened to them; they were terrified of repercussions.

For so many years we had all heard the stories of how people regarded as dangerous by the government just disappeared. Whenever I spoke to black people it was always behind closed doors, never in public places, and they always talked in low voices and incessantly looked over their shoulders. Basically, Zimbabwe had become a nation of people terrified of their own government with everyone believing that silence was the only assurance of safety.

The silence of all the local people who lived around Stow Farm had been a permanent feature for me and I spent many, many hours agonising over the reasons my friends, both black and white, had for not speaking out. In my heart I knew it was pure fear, but undoubtedly there were other reasons to explain the silence of black Zimbabweans. Perhaps some had been sucked in by the government propaganda spewing out incessant rhetoric that all whites were bad, imperialist, neo-colonialist racists. Perhaps they, like so many others, did not want to be seen talking to whites for fear of being called sell-outs. Or perhaps, for a time, they had thought that they themselves might get a piece of Stow Farm. This was not as unlikely as it sounded. A friend in Harare managing a big engineering company had recently told me the most bizarre story of how one of his employees had asked for a day off work so that he could go and claim his new piece of land. When asked where the land was situated, the man had replied: 'Oh, on Stow Farm in Marondera.'

Even more obscene had been meeting my long-standing black friends who owned a small farm just outside Marondera. Going to visit them on their farm for tea on a Sunday afternoon I asked where all their sheep and dairy cows had gone. 'They're on the new farm,' I was told. After exclaiming with delight that they had got a new farm, I was absolutely horrified to be told that they hadn't bought it but had been allocated the farm by the government. These wealthy people, both from very influential families, had applied for land even though they already had a farm of their own. It didn't matter how I looked at it, I just could not see why they should be beneficiaries of a scheme that was supposedly taking land from white people and giving it to landless black peasants. They were a two-car family, their son went to an exclusive private boarding school, and they enjoyed a very good lifestyle.

I wanted to push my chair back and leave right there and then, but did not trust my legs to hold me up. Then, with more than a few beers under their belts, these old friends of my family told me that they were having some trouble in getting the white farmer and his family out of the house. I was horrified to think that this highly educated, upper-class family could have done something like this, particularly as they had been so angry, outspoken and supportive when war veterans had chased my family off Stow Farm. Just two years earlier, they had begged me not to give in to the bunch of thugs squatting on Stow Farm. 'Just burn the buggers out,' they had said of the war veterans, insisting that they would never let anyone chase them off their little farm. Now they had betrayed both our friendship and all their principles and climbed onto the government bandwagon. All week they were business executives earning much more money than I ever could, and on the weekends they became war veterans.

I was so upset that I struggled to find any words and just kept asking: 'How could you?' but there was no answer, no explanation for what I saw as plain greed. They both told me I was being too emotional about it all and reasoned that if something was being given out for free by the government, why not take advantage of it?

'But what about all the people losing everything they've worked for all their lives? What about all the farm workers and their families and the white man and his wife and kids?' I asked. 'What do you think you are doing to their lives? Or is it OK because they are white and you are black?'

There was no answer, but we all knew that their land grab had nothing whatsoever to do with race. It was just greed.

'And what if it had been Stow Farm you had been allocated?' I asked. 'Would you have been the war vets shouting at me through the farm gate ordering me to get off my land? My God, what if you'd been given Stow?'

The answer to my question was immediate, but it was whispered with shame and without eye contact: 'God help us, Cath!'

I was sickened and so very sad that this had become the face of Zimbabwe. What my black friends had been sucked into and gone along with was totally inexcusable. I do not know how you live with yourself after having done something like this; how you sleep at night knowing that your actions have hurt so many other people. I wondered if they would ever think about what became of the white farmer and his family or all the farm workers and their families in the years ahead. I wondered how, or if, they would ever tell their children how they acquired their new farm. I did not know if the damage to this long-time friendship could ever be repaired, or indeed if I even wanted it to be.

I knew that the actions of my black friends in grabbing a white-owned farm and chasing out the legal owners was not representative of the majority of Zimbabweans. I also knew that the reason most people did not speak out against injustice was because of personal fear and not guilt. For 27 months the businessmen and traders around Stow Farm had allowed themselves to sit in cocooned silence, had been too scared to tell me what they knew or had seen. Now that the horror of a squatter camp had arrived on their own doorstep and was directly affecting their own lives, health and businesses, they couldn't wait to tell me everything. Over the next few days I pieced together the story of what had really happened on Stow Farm in the weeks following its takeover by a man called Wind and his three friends some six weeks before.

Two days after I had visited the Marondera District Administrator and told him that a bunch of thugs had taken over our farm and moved into the homestead, four vehicles had turned into the gateway of Stow Farm. In the first truck were 'The Boys'. These men were, according to eyewitnesses, well-known war veterans from the Marondera and Murehwa areas. They got out and stood near their vehicle, their presence and stance threatening and very intimidating. In the second car was the District Administrator himself, with his minder and another man. Behind that was a police Land Rover with armed details and behind them a truckload of men from the Police Support Unit, armed and in riot gear.

The District Administrator called Wind and his friends out of the farmhouse. 'Who are you people?' he barked. 'What do you think you are doing here? Who gave you permission to take over this house?'

'We are in charge of this farm,' they replied. 'The war veterans told us to come here. We have come to take our land back from the whites.'

'I do not know any of you,' the DA spat back at them. 'I have not seen your faces in my office. No war veterans have given you permission to do this. I have not seen your application forms for land. Who gave you permission to be here? Who told you to come here and just take this place?'

'But we heard so on the ZBC radio and at the rallies,' one of the men said. 'We were told that we should chase the farmers off their land and take back what is ours. The government told us at the election rallies: "Go and settle yourselves! Take back what the whites have stolen from you and your ancestors!" The government of Robert Gabriel Mugabe told us to do this!'

'That was just politics!' the DA said. 'Just politics for the elections.'

The men who had occupied the house on Stow Farm were then given a long, loud and very angry lecture by the DA, and told to immediately hand over all the keys and surrender themselves to the waiting police. The eyewitnesses watching from a safe distance said that the keys were handed over but the men did not give themselves up, they took to their heels and ran into the bush. Two were caught, handcuffed and arrested by the Support Unit. The other two put up a fight and were beaten badly. One of these men died a few days later.

With Wind and his friends taken care of, the keys to all the buildings and gates on Stow Farm were handed over to the war veterans accompanying the DA. For two days everything went quiet on Stow Farm, and then huge lorries started arriving and disgorged 100 people and their belongings. These people had been evicted by police from a farm they had been occupying on the other side of Marondera. They had been evicted because that farm had been earmarked for a government minister who did not want his newly acquired property littered with squatters. They had all their worldly goods with them, including blankets, pots, pans, buckets and watering cans. They had thatching grass to make new shelters with, bags of maize and groundnuts that they had reaped from their previous squat and a few goats and chickens.

These 100 squatters got the best accommodation on offer and moved into the tobacco barns and grading sheds on Stow Farm. The next day the lorries returned and dumped more people who had been evicted from another Marondera farm that had been allocated to a senior government official. They came with sheets of tin and wheelbarrows, bags of nyimo beans and buckets of onions and sweet potatoes. Some had ducks and scrawny domestic dogs, and they all had to find a place for themselves on Stow Farm. They moved into the remaining houses in the workers' village and into the dairy, milking parlour and milk cooling room.

Two days later more squatters were dumped on Stow Farm. They had four cattle, five goats and two pigs, and moved into the bulk feed storerooms adjoining the dairy. Some erected shelters at either end of what had been the dipping spray race and used the poles from the cattle crush to build more shelters. When still more trucks arrived with people there was no room left and so they erected shacks down the driveway and throughout the gum plantation. Each family was allocated a space of four square metres for their house and a further four square metres in which to cook and wash. When there were 20 shacks in a line down the driveway and yet more people were dumped on the farm, they squabbled for space and the war veterans in the 'big house' came and paced out lines amongst the gum trees.

Locals in the area told me that between 500 and 700 people had been dumped on Stow Farm in a period of ten days. All were people who had been occupying and squatting on farms that had been taken from white commercial farmers and given to government officials in what Agriculture Minister Made had called the A2 phase of land redistribution. The people were all told that they were being left on Stow Farm temporarily; they were in transit to somewhere, but no one knew to where. They were all told that they would be moved in a few days' time, but the days passed and then the weeks, and still no one came for them.

The dumped squatters settled into some sort of a routine, but their new existence was abominable. There were only three pit latrines in the area and there was no piped water, as the borehole motor had long since been burned out. They queued from dusk to dawn at the well in the yard of the butchery over the road for drinking water and walked down through the fields to wash themselves, their children and their clothes in the little stock dam. The villagers and local businessmen surrounding Stow Farm told me that when the women walked down to the dam in the morning there were so many children with them that it looked like two bus-loads on a school expedition. They say that there are at least 200 children amongst the dumped squatters on the farm.

I asked people how the squatters were surviving and what they were eating. I was told that little by little they were selling their possessions to people who wait on the corner for buses – a goat or chicken, a cup of maize or handful of ground nuts or nyimo beans. The local people are not buying the squatters' goods, though, they say they have seen the conditions in the camp and the piles of human faeces that are everywhere amongst the trees.

'You can't foot it in there,' one man told me, laughing and shaking his head. 'Aah no, you cannot walk in there, the shit is everywhere.'

'Sure!' another exclaimed. 'It is everywhere and the stink is terrible. And the children, we feel such shame for the children. They are so dirty and always they have the shit on their feet and between their toes, on their legs and on their clothes. It is terrible for sure and people are going to die.'

'Two have already died,' a man said, 'an old man and a young woman. Maybe it is cholera, we don't know, but it is going to be serious and for sure we won't buy their things.'

'Hah! Even to shake their hands is not all right,' the woman said. 'Maybe we can catch cholera.'

The talk went on and on, the stories of horror and depravity poured out and I did not know how to cope with the flood of emotions that filled my senses. The people who had been dumped on Stow Farm were all men and women who had been squatting on other farms for over two years. They had all been ignorant and gullible enough to believe that they would be allowed to stay on the farms they had occupied. It was hard for me to feel sorry for them or their plight, but I could not help pitying the 200 innocent children who were cold, filthy and starving because their parents had allowed themselves to be used and moved around like pawns on a chess board.

'What can we do now?' I asked. 'Can we just sit here and let those people starve and die?'

The response of all the people I spoke to was unanimous. 'We must do nothing! Those people there on your farm must learn that this government does not care for her people. They must learn how cruel their leaders are. They must see now that this government never keeps its promises. They must suffer now so that they learn and will never vote for this party again.'

There is no doubt that the months and years ahead will be filled with hunger and suffering for millions of Zimbabweans. As I sit and write this last paragraph there is no salt, sugar, maize meal, cooking oil or flour in the country. Eggs and milk are getting harder to find and bread shortages are imminent. I, like thousands of others, do not believe that this is the end of Zimbabwe, and I continually delay making a decision to leave the country of my birth. I am too scared to go, but also very scared of staying. I know this will end and that when it does there will be so much to do, so many wounds to heal – and so much promise for the future.

*

On 2 September 2002, President Mugabe stood in front of world leaders and thousands of delegates at the World Summit for Sustainable Development in Sandton, Johannesburg. In clear and defiant terms the 78-year-old Zimbabwean president lashed out at the world in general and Britain in particular. '… So Blair, keep your England and let me keep my Zimbabwe,' he said. Mugabe accused Britain of wanting to reclaim Zimbabwe, saying Britain had repeatedly broken its promises to fund land reform in Zimbabwe and was trying to interfere in issues which undermined Zimbabwe's sovereignty.

Wisely, Tony Blair chose not to enter into a war of words with Mugabe at the Summit, but he later reiterated what Britain's policy was with regard to giving Zimbabwe money for land reform:

> … The money is there for land reform. He could get that money and use it for land reform – because land reform is necessary – at any point in time [that] he wanted. The only demand that has been made is that it is done through the UN programme, in order to make sure that the money goes to the poor people that actually need it and not into the pockets of him and his henchmen and the other people running the show.

Contrary to well-documented and unopposed evidence that the pick of Zimbabwe's farms were being seized and given to government ministers, army personnel and senior government supporters, Mugabe again attempted to hoodwink the world about land ownership and redistribution in the country:

… We have said even as we acquire land, [that] we shall not deprive the white farmers of rights completely. Every one of them is entitled to at least one farm. But they would want to continue to have more than one farm. More than one farm indeed. Fifteen, 20, 35 farms for one person … No farmer is being left without land … We are threatening no one … We wish no harm to anyone; we are Zimbabweans, we are Africans.

In direct contradiction to his Summit speech President Mugabe arrived back in Zimbabwe and spoke at Harare airport. Speaking in general about white farmers who were contesting the acquisition of their farms, Mugabe said: '… Those do not deserve to be in Zimbabwe and we shall take steps to ensure that they are not entitled to our land.' In the same speech and this time with reference to white farmer and opposition MP Roy Bennett and leading lawyer and opposition MP David Coltart, Mugabe said:

… The Bennetts and the Coltarts are not part of our society. They belong to Britain and let them go there. If they want to stay here, we will say 'stay' but your place is in jail.

President Mugabe's words at both the World Summit and Harare airport may have been filled with vitriolic rhetoric, but he clearly meant what he said. Mugabe's speech at the World Summit slamming both Britain and Tony Blair had been met with applause and cheers.

Zimbabweans were not alone in expressing shock at the applause Mugabe had garnered at the Summit but it was a confusing message. In my perhaps naïve way, I saw the applause as being not so much for Mugabe's words as for his daring in speaking out against the West, and against one of the world's most powerful leaders.

The politics aside, the situation on the ground in Zimbabwe in early September 2002 was diabolical. During the last fortnight of August, over 250 commercial farmers were arrested for refusing to obey government warnings that all farmers should vacate their land by the end of that month. Even farmers, who had official documentation from the courts stating that the acquisition of their properties had been overthrown, were arrested.

In the days that followed, farmers were released on bail with conditions that varied enormously from one part of the country to another. Some were ordered by magistrates to leave their farms within 24 hours, others were given a week or a month and still others were told that they should not leave their farms at all, as the processes leading to their arrest had been illegal.

Yet, in some of the smaller areas the farmers were left completely alone and it seemed to be the direct result of the degree of hostility and vigour being employed by local politicians, war veterans, district administrators and police members in charge.

Obtaining the figures of exactly how many farmers had left their properties by early September 2002 was not easy but it appears that over 50% left. Some went to nearby towns and cities where property prices were soaring due to demand, and finding accommodation became almost impossible. Many farmers with children said they would stay in the towns until the end of the school year and just wait and see what was going to happen. Others put in visa applications and made plans to leave Zimbabwe.

The fate of an estimated 1,5 million displaced black farm workers remains a major tragedy. The International Crisis Group co-director John Prendergast said that farm workers were being left 'literally homeless and desperate' and were simply falling through the cracks of the crisis.

On 10 September 2002, MDC leader Morgan Tsvangirai addressed a public seminar in Harare. He attacked the complete breakdown of Zimbabawe's democratic process. Tsvangirai said that the government's policies had reduced the majority of the population to the economic level of Stone Age scavengers. Tsvangirai reportedly promised to rededicate himself to mobilising the MDC supporters and to continue his struggle for democracy and good governance in Zimbabwe.

As a nation we looked to him for hope; there was none anywhere else.

Cathy Buckle
10 September 2002

APPENDIX

This is a chronological list of some of the events that have taken place in Zimbabwe from December 2001 to May 2002. On many occasions the dates noted are those on which the events were reported in the media. The list is far from complete and includes almost none of the gross human rights violations that have ravaged our country since February 2000 when Zanu PF lost a constitutional referendum. It shows how President Mugabe and his Zanu PF party were determined to stay in power at any cost, how they changed the laws, ignored court judgements, introduced repressive legislation and used presidential edicts, decrees and powers to ensure their continued governance of Zimbabwe. This list reveals:

- blatantly obvious connections between violence and elections – whether ward, council, mayoral, parliamentary or presidential;
- the gradual and sustained attack on freedom of the press, and freedom of speech and expression;
- sustained harassment of the legal and judicial structures of the country and how judges partial to Zanu PF were put into the system;
- how our defence forces and police were infiltrated by war veterans who were promoted to superior ranks;
- the ruthless attack on an opposition party that holds 58 seats in Parliament;
- how anyone who supported the MDC was hounded, whether Members of Parliament or men and women in rural villages;
- how everyone working for democracy was chased from their

homes, beaten, tortured, and had their possessions destroyed or their relations murdered;
• how a once-thriving nation and regional food exporter became ostracised from the world;
• that Zimbabwe's descent into starvation has never been about land and race, but about politics.

JANUARY 2001

1   MDC supporter Bernard Gara is murdered in Bikita West.
13-14 By-elections held in Bikita West are won by Zanu PF.
16   Democratic Republic of Congo President Laurent Kabila is assassinated.
26   133 farms are listed for compulsory acquisition by government.
28   Z$100 million printing presses of the *Daily News* are bombed.
31   One person is murdered in political violence in January 2001.

FEBRUARY 2001

3   Riot police break up a peaceful demonstration by journalists in Harare protesting the bombing of the *Daily News*.
9   Police have still made no arrests in connection with *Daily News* bombing; government begins to pressurise Supreme Court Chief Justice Gubbay to resign.
14   Armed men in army uniform storm the house of MDC MP Job Sikhala and assault him and his pregnant wife.
16   War veterans arrive en masse in Masvingo ahead of mayoral elections.
22   Foreign journalist Mercedes Sayagues and BBC Correspondent Joseph Winter, both resident in Zimbabwe, are declared prohibited immigrants and ordered to leave the country; people suspected to be war veterans attempt to break into the home of journalist Joseph Winter; CIO agents attempt to break into the home of Loice Matanda-Moyo, an officer in the Attorney General's Office who had granted an order extending the departure date of journalist Joseph Winter.
27   Senior Police Assistant Commissioner Solomon Ncube resigns from the force.

28   One person is murdered in political violence in February 2001.

MARCH 2001

1   In an annual report figures show that tourist arrivals have shrunk by 60 per cent and over 5 000 people have been made redundant in the sector in the past year.

2   Soldiers are unleashed in Chitungwiza and other high-density suburbs around Harare; numerous civilians are severely assaulted over a number of days; war veteran shareholders of ZEXCOM call for the arrest of Chenjerai Hunzvi over fraud allegations amounting to Z$50 million.

4   Commercial farmer Gloria Olds, aged 72, is shot 15 times at her gate shortly after dawn, her dogs are killed and her car is used as a getaway vehicle.

6   Inyathi farmer Denis Streak is abducted and held for a number of hours by war veterans.

7   Armed men claiming to be war veterans shoot and seriously injure Trust Moyo and David Mota in Epworth outside Harare; police have still made no arrests in connection with the bombing of the *Daily News* printing presses and have released no information on the matter.

8   Zanu PF-supporting judge, Godfrey Chidyausiku, is appointed Acting Chief Justice of the Supreme Court; Zanu PF MP Eddison Zvobgo accuses Zanu PF of introducing unconstitutional and irrational laws governing broadcasting in Zimbabwe; armed war veterans invade an Harare estate agency and assault the managing director; High Court hears sworn testimony that Olivia Muchena (MP for Mutoko South) told people at a rally that anyone who supported the MDC would be killed.

9   The Midlands Chamber of Zimbabwe Industries (CZI) reports that 1 000 workers have been retrenched in the last two months in the Midlands.

19   Zimbabwe Republic Police promote 300 war veterans to ranks of Sergeant & Assistant Inspector.

20   A delegation from the Committee to Protect Journalists meets with Zimbabwe's ambassador to the USA.

22   Exiled Ethiopian dictator Mengistu Haile Mariam and his

family are given permanent resident status in Zimbabwe; inflation hits 57,7 per cent.

23   War veterans storm the Harare Children's Home, shout, threaten and demand to see the supervisor; they also invade more than a dozen other Harare businesses under the guise of resolving labour disputes; 95 farms are listed for compulsory acquisition.

26   War veterans and Zanu PF supporters close down Bulawayo textile company Dezign Inc.

28   500 000 people register for food aid in the Masvingo province; war veterans and Zanu PF supporters invade companies in Kadoma.

29   Masvingo Provincial Governor Josiah Hungwe threatens Masvingo residents with death if they do not vote for Zanu PF in mayoral elections.

31   Harare Hospital reports that it has run out of essential drugs; nine infant deaths are being recorded per week at the hospital; 80 per cent of children admitted are suffering from malnutrition; five people are murdered in political violence in March 2001.

APRIL 2001

2   Nurses and health workers in Nkayi, suspected of supporting the MDC, are dismissed and replaced by army personnel.

4   Chenjerai Hunzvi announces that war veterans will set up base centres in all urban centres; teachers are forced to pay protection money to war veterans in Mashonaland East.

9   Zimbabwean lawyers petition Police Commissioner Chihuri to stop police harassment of lawyers; University of Zimbabwe (UZ) first-year student Batanai Hadzizi dies after being assaulted by riot police.

10   Riot police fire shrapnel-loaded tear gas at UZ students who march in peaceful protest through Harare; war veteran Joseph Chinotimba declares himself the president of the Zimbabwe Congress of Trade Unions; war veterans and Zanu PF supporters invade and close the Chipinge branch of Farm and City Centre.

12   War veterans and Zanu PF supporters assault five senior

officials at the Cotton Company of Zimbabwe's Gokwe branch; hundreds of villagers from the Kezi district flee to the mountains to escape rampaging war veterans and government supporters incensed at the locals' support of an MDC rally.

18 President Mugabe threatens to nationalise mines and manufacturing companies that are closing down due to economic collapse.

20 Two Pakistani businessmen who have invested Z$200 million in Zimbabwe flee the country after repeated attacks by war veterans on their city businesses and homes; 137 farms are listed for compulsory acquisition by the government.

24 War veterans and Zanu PF supporters invade the Harare Avenues Clinic, Macsteel Zimbabwe, Meikles department store and the Forestry Commission; they also force the Dental Clinic to pay out Z$7 million, and the company closes completely.

25 War veterans and Zanu PF supporters invade Mechman Engineering and successfully demand pay-outs to employees of Z$7 million; they also invade Resource Drilling, Trinidad Industries, Lobels Bakery, Scotco, Omnia Fertilizer, Leno Trading, Willdale Bricks, Madel Training Centre, Craster and Phillips.

26 South Africa summons the Zimbabwe High Commissioner and protests the violent attacks on its businesses in Harare; Chenjerai Hunzvi warns that war veterans will target foreign embassies and NGOs in the ongoing company invasions; the EU protests to the Zimbabwe government about war veterans who raid and steal Z$1 million worth of food aid given to victims of Cyclone Eline; the Law Society urges Justice Minister Chinamasa to end attacks against lawyers; a seven-member panel of international jurists releases a report criticising attacks against Zimbabwe's judiciary.

27 Agriculture Minister Joseph Made insists that there will be no food shortages in Zimbabwe and no need to import any wheat or maize; 374 farms are listed for compulsory acquisition by the government – included are the country's major tea and coffee estates.

28   Still no arrests three months after *Daily News* press
        bombings; Minister of Youth, Border Gezi, dies in a car
        crash.

30   Red Cross and Red Crescent Societies move their seven
        expatriate families out of Zimbabwe, fearing for their safety.

MAY 2001

1   War veteran Joseph Chinotimba invades May Day
        celebrations and takes over the proceedings, says
        companies in Bulawayo will be named for invasions by his
        colleagues.

4   Economists predict that Z$8,5 billion will be needed to
        import grain into Zimbabwe; 40 farms are listed for
        compulsory acquisition by the government; MDC activists
        are kidnapped and beaten in Masvingo

6   Riot police seal off high-density suburbs in Masvingo as
        political violence breaks out. MDC supporters are arrested
        and have their car impounded.

8   Agriculture Minister Joseph Made announces that all wheat
        exports have immediately been suspended. Made continues
        to insist that wheat stocks are adequate and no grain will
        have to be imported; violent clashes take place in Masvingo
        between MDC and Zanu PF supporters led by Chenjerai
        Hunzvi, and 13 people are injured.

10   The British Council closes its Library and Information
        Department Offices in Harare for safety reasons; the World
        Press Freedom Campaign urges the Zimbabwe government
        to ensure the safety of journalists; Information Minister
        Jonathan Moyo says government will not order a halt to
        company invasions by war veterans.

11   Eighty-one farms are listed for compulsory acquisition by
        the government; the world-famous Gonarezhou National
        Park, which is state-owned land, is demarcated into plots
        for agricultural resettlement; the French ambassador to
        Zimbabwe publicly condemns invasions of companies by
        war veterans.

14   Mayoral elections in Masvingo are won by the MDC
        candidate.

16   War veterans invade Speciss College in Harare.

18   Some war veterans are arrested on charges of invading companies, but their leaders are not touched, in what is seen as a cover up operation; one of those arrested, Mike Moyo, says Chinotimba and Hunzvi have benefited financially from the invasions and threatens to reveal them; Mike Moyo is released from police custody; 19 farms are listed for compulsory acquisition by the government.

24   The Danish embassy suspends Z$100 million aid for private sector partnerships in Zimbabwe; Chenjerai Hunzvi is said to be recovering in hospital after collapsing in Bulawayo; the war veterans association denies reports that Hunzvi has died.

25   Chenjerai Hunzvi is transferred to Parirenyatwa Hospital in Harare and said to be suffering from malaria.

26   Defence Minister Moven Mahachi dies in a car crash near Nyanga; five other people in the car at the time only sustain minor injuries.

27   MDC council election candidate is kidnapped and assaulted by Zanu PF supporters; he still wins the election in Plumtree for the MDC.

29   Zanu PF supporters attack six homes, burn possessions and assault people they suspect of supporting the MDC in Bindura; the CFU says maize production has dropped by 43 per cent and predicts a deficit of 600 000 tonnes.

30   US Secretary of State, Colin Powell, speaks out strongly against President Mugabe and urges South Africa to do likewise.

31   Government officials including police, CIO and municipal workers are implicated in a land scam in which resettled people paid them Z$10 million in order to be allocated plots of land in Matabeleland; the CFU withdraws all litigation against the government and announces the formation of the Zimbabwe Joint Resettlement Initiative with Z$1 billion offered in aid for resettled people; three people are murdered in political violence in May 2001.

JUNE 2001

4   War veteran leader Chenjerai 'Hitler' Hunzvi dies aged 51.

7   War veterans invade the property of black commercial farmer Philemon Matibe who was the MDC candidate for

Chegutu and whose contesting of the 2000 parliamentary election results in court is due to commence within days; Mr Matibe is forced to vacate the farm and dismiss his workers.

8   Twenty-seven farms in Macheke are not operating due to war veterans enforcing work stoppages.

9   War veterans invade the Beatrice Country Club. Farmers holding a cricket match are accused of celebrating the death of Chenjerai Hunzvi. War veterans chase all patrons away, consume all the food and alcohol and rename the premises the Chenjerai Hitler Hunzvi Club.
Police refuse to act.

12   The Bulawayo branch of the CZI reports that 400 companies have closed and 100 000 people have been made jobless due to continuing economic decline.

13   War veterans vandalise Z$100 million of irrigation equipment and Z$50 million of property on farms in Masvingo.

14   Petrol, diesel, paraffin and aviation fuel prices rise by 70 per cent.

15   A 50-year-old female Australian aid worker is assaulted by war veterans for walking past the house where mourners of Chenjerai Hunzvi were gathered; the Agricultural Workers Union reports that only three out of every 500 people being resettled on seized farms are farm workers and says that many thousands face destitution.

17   Farm worker Zondiwa Dumukani is beaten to death with golf clubs by government supporters in front of numerous eyewitnesses and a ZBC television camera crew; war veterans burn tobacco seed beds on seven properties, one of which reports loss to the value of Z$42 million. The Tobacco Association reports that 80 tobacco farms have been prevented from planting a crop, representing a loss of 19 per cent of the country's total harvest.

18   BBC documentary producer Sean Langan is ordered out of the country; eight headmen, 25 teachers and two headmasters are fired by war veterans in Buhera and ordered to leave the area.

19   A BBC TV crew (Simon Finch, John Sweeney and James

Miller) are ordered out of Zimbabwe by Information Minister Jonathan Moyo.

20   Ministry of Education officials tell teachers fired by war veterans in Buhera that if they do not resolve their political differences with war veterans they will be struck off the payroll.

22   421 farms are listed for compulsory acquisition by government. Included is the farm belonging to murdered farmers Martin and Gloria Olds. Also listed are missions owned by the Catholic Church, land owned by the Cold Storage Company and the National Railways.

26   35 people are injured when government supporters descend on a gold mine in Shamva, beat people and destroy property, accusing the mine owners of allowing NCA (Constitutional Assembly) meetings to be held there; scores of villagers, MDC activists and NCA members flee their homes in Guruve after being attacked by government supporters who accuse them of supporting the MDC.

28   The EU gives the Zimbabwe government 60 days to end violence and farm occupations, abolish curbs on the media and uphold court rulings, or face tough penalties.

29   An 18-page supplement to the *Herald* newspaper lists another 2 030 farms which have been gazetted for compulsory acquisition by the government: 90 per cent of farming properties in the country are now listed for seizure; UK *Daily Telegraph* journalist David Blair is ordered to leave Zimbabwe.

30   Sixty war veterans armed with axes and broken bottles barricade the Marondera Hotel and prevent an NCA meeting from being held there; one person is murdered in political violence in June 2001.

JULY 2001

2   Armed war veterans evict a family from their home in Waterfalls in Harare, saying they are going to settle on the premises; the Supreme Court rules four to one that the government's Fast Track Land Resettlement Scheme is illegal and that no more Section 5 or 8 letters should be issued.

5   Author George Mujajati is severely assaulted in his home by armed men in army uniform for not going to work due to the nationwide stayaway called by the ZCTU; armed soldiers beat people indiscriminately in five Harare high-density suburbs for the same reason; farming industry experts say that farm output will decline by 90 per cent and 300 000 farm workers will become destitute if the government goes ahead with the seizure of all farms listed for acquisition.

6   New Chief Justice Chidyausiku says that previous Supreme Court rulings against the government's land reform programme were incorrect, four judges in the Supreme Court disagree with the judgement; legislation is gazetted barring dual nationality in Zimbabwe: people who were born in Zimbabwe but whose parents were not are required to renounce any claims to citizenship by ancestry of any other country; 20 000 war veterans are given backdated allowances by the government for their role in land seizures after representation was made by Joseph Chinotimba to Zanu PF.

9   Commercial farmer Iain Kay is barricaded into his home by war veterans and government supporters.

12   Libyan leader Moammar Gadaffi arrives in a 50-vehicle motorcade in Zimbabwe and at a series of impromptu gatherings urges people to fight for land and says Africa has no place for white people; Agritex officials report that almost half a million people are facing starvation and need urgent food aid in the Midlands province; Zanu PF youths and war veterans begin a reign of terror in Bindura ahead of by-elections. Many schools are closed after teachers flee and reports of children being raped and people beaten escalate; Finance Minister Simba Makoni confirms that Zimbabwe is facing severe food shortages, in direct contradiction to pronouncements made by Agriculture Minister Made.

13   Gazetting of 529 farms for compulsory acquisition by the government.

14   Odzi farmer Philip Bezuidenhout runs over and kills a man on the road near his property; on reporting it to the police

he is arrested, imprisoned and charged with murder, but it is four days before police inspect the scene of the accident; 60 Zanu PF youths led by Joseph Chinotimba establish bases in Bindura and assault scores of people whom they accuse of supporting the MDC; 27 MDC youths are taken by police and dumped in the bush 150 km away.

17   The farm and home of farmer Philip Bezuidenhout is broken into and looted by war veterans; two other farmhouses in the neighbourhood are looted and many farmers evacuate their properties.

18   UN Secretary General Kofi Annan says that land reform in Zimbabwe must be handled in a legal and transparent manner; Gwanda South Zanu PF MP is implicated in game poaching on ranches in the area: a man is apprehended while driving the MP's car with a kudu carcass in it, but the MP is not available for comment.

19   All non-commissioned army and police officers who served in the liberation war are promoted a rank higher; Manicaland Provincial Governor Oppah Muchinguri expels reporters from the *Daily News* and *Financial Gazette* from a meeting being held to discuss land resettlement. Reporters from the ZBC and *Herald* are allowed to stay at the meeting.

22   Several people are injured, five seriously, and a vehicle burnt when an MDC motorcade carrying Morgan Tsvangirai is attacked outside Bindura.

23   The Horticulture Promotion Council say that earnings have dropped by Z$275 million.

27   Former US Ambassador to the UN, Andrew Young, says that the violence and killing in Zimbabwe must stop; Jack Salim, on the police wanted list for 14 cases of robbery and violence, is a leading member of the Zanu PF campaigning team for the Bindura by-election; police confirm that Salim had been arrested but was released on instruction of senior Zanu PF officials.

30   A High Court Judge orders Police Commissioner Chihuri, the Governor of Mashonaland East, the officer in charge of Marondera Police, the CIO, District Administrators and Provincial Administrators to act against invaders overrunning Iain Kay's farm; the Zimbabwe Human Rights

Forum releases a report entitled 'Who Was Responsible' for the political violence in 2000. Victims are accounted for as follows: MDC – 609; Unknown political affiliation – 63; Zanu PF – 5. 644 perpetrators are named as 'alleged to have personally taken part in, been present or in some way sanctioned' acts of political violence. Alleged perpetrators include Zanu PF parliamentary candidates: Chenjerai Hunzvi, Gladys Hokoyo, Sabina Thembani, Shadreck Chipangu, Border Gezi, Chen Chimutengwende, Chistopher Kuruneri, Nicholas Goche, Nobbie Dzinzi, Saviour Kasukwere, David Chapfiki, Herbert Murerwa, Joel Matiza, Joseph Ray Kaukonde and Mark Madiro.

31   Five people are murdered in political violence in July 2001.

AUGUST 2001

1   Outgoing president of the CFU, Tim Henwood, gives a final speech which reports: maize production is down by more than half; cotton production has shrunk by almost half; the tobacco crop is down by 20 per cent; 60 per cent of dairy farms have been listed for government seizure; wildlife populations on safari farms are being depleted.

2   An Israeli company is contracted to provide Z$1 billion worth of special vehicles, water cannons and other riot gear for the Zimbabwe government.

3   Kwekwe farmer Ralph Corbett is axed by war veterans on his farm and is on life support systems in a Harare hospital; a World Bank study reports that it will take 15 years for full productivity to be reached in Zimbabwe's land reform programme; 350 war veterans peg plots in the middle of a winter wheat crop on Peter Goosen's farm in Matabeleland North.

5   Minister of Local Government Ignatius Chombo and Chinoyi Zanu PF MP Philip Chiyangwa visit war veterans on farms in Chinoyi.

6   Axed farmer Ralph Corbett dies; 22 farmers are arrested in Chinoyi after some had clashed with war veterans while attempting to rescue their neighbour whose door was being axed open; six of the people arrested were not involved in the clashes and another six had simply gone to the police

station to enquire about their colleagues; all the farmers are remanded in custody.

7   At least ten white people are assaulted in the streets of Chinoyi by government supporters

9   Forty farming families in Chinoyi evacuate their homes as war veterans go on the rampage in the area; reports of looting, burning and beating are rife.

11   Ten farms in Doma, Lions Den and Mhangura are looted by war veterans and government supporters; reports from the CFU say that Z$1 billion worth of buildings and property had been destroyed and 4 000 farm workers face joblessness; newspapers report that police vehicles were used in the looting spree.

12   Vice President Joseph Msika is on record as saying that 'whites are not human beings'.

13   War veterans and Agritex officers peg and partition plots on MDC MP Roy Bennet's Chimanimani coffee farm.

14   *Daily News* editors Geoff Nyarota, Bill Saidi and John Gambanga are taken into police custody for publishing reports that police vehicles had been used in the Chinoyi farm lootings.

16   The *Herald* newspaper reports that white farmers in Chinoyi, together with the British, had looted their own farms in an attempt to destabilise the country and prompt international intervention.

17   War veteran Joseph Chinotimba is in court on charges of attempted murder.

18   Agriculture Minister Joseph Made announces in the *Herald* that all white farmers should immediately vacate their properties to allow settlers to move in.

20   Masvingo police refuse to obey a magistrate's ruling to hand over 50 soldiers who had gone on the rampage and assaulted numerous people in the area; a High Court judge orders the immediate release on bail of 22 Chinoyi farmers in custody for 14 days.

22   Matabeleland commercial farmer Peter Goosen is given a 24-hour deadline to vacate his property by 100 war veterans and government supporters; a *Daily News* reporter covering the story is assaulted with sticks and knobkerries while

police look on; war veteran Joseph Chinotimba says that he will close down the offices of all independent newspapers if they continue to publish reports about divisions amongst war veterans; editor of the *Standard* newspaper, Mark Chavunduka, is arrested for publishing reports that President Mugabe was being haunted by the ghost of Josiah Tongogara.

23 Scores of farm workers and villagers in Chinoyi confirm police involvement in the looting of farms in the area.

24 War veterans invade a Harare farm given to the late First Lady, Sally Mugabe. The property was to be used for a Children's Home for street children but war veterans demarcate and sell plots to settlers who arrive en masse in trucks; 20 farms in Hwedza are stopped from operating by war veterans; 35 000 farm workers and their families are chased out of their homes and are camped on roadsides.

25 Twenty-four families accused of being MDC supporters flee their homes and villages in Mount Darwin; a magistrate's order to Bindura police to facilitate the return of the families is not complied with.

27 Two senior police officials are suspended and a number of prison officials are being investigated for giving imprisoned Chinoyi farmers jackets and blankets.

30 Reports are released detailing profits of US$300 million in a deal between Zanu PF and the Democratic Republic of Congo involving the logging of 33 million hectares of rainforest in the DRC.

31 Seventy-two-year-old Mvurwi farmer, Wessel Weller, his wife and six employees are assaulted by 50 war veterans and government supporters; talks are held between Libya and Zimbabwe about fuel procurement, newspapers report that Libya wants shareholdings in Zimbabwe's oil company (NOCZIM) in exchange for fuel; a Z$4 billion beef deal with Libya is in jeopardy due to the outbreak of foot and mouth disease in Zimbabwe; two people are murdered in political violence in August 2001.

SEPTEMBER 2001

6 An agreement is made in Abuja, Nigeria, between the

Zimbabwean and British governments: a communique is signed in which the Zimbabwe government agrees to no more illegal land seizures, taking firm action against violence and intimidation on farms and abiding by Zimbabwe's own laws; in exchange the British will pay £35 million towards compensating white farmers and encourage the donor community to assist in land reform programmes in Zimbabwe; two MDC polling agents are abducted and beaten ahead of mayoral elections; the CFU reports that 900 farms are not operating owing to land invasions.

7   Listing of 110 farms for compulsory acquisition by the government.

8   Masvingo Provincial Governor Josiah Hungwe approves the resettlement of 600 families in the world-renowned Gonarezhou National Park; 30 war veterans attack workers on Iain Kay's farm, and burn property and homes.

11   A headmaster in Chikomba is bludgeoned to death by war veterans who accuse him of supporting the MDC.

13   A High Court judge again orders Police Commissioner Chihuri to instruct police to evict invaders on Iain Kay's farm; MDC Ward Chairman for Chikomba is severely assaulted by police and then released into the custody of Zanu PF youths who beat him further; Minister of Local Government Ignatius Chombo accuses white farmers of deliberately starting fires and burning their own land.

17   Three *Daily News* reporters are attacked by war veterans with fists, chains and poles on John Bibby's Wedza farm.

26   Zanu PF supporters invade three gold mines in the Midlands and steal concentrates worth millions.

27   The Minister of Health tells Parliament that there are only 14 doctors and 105 nurses left in government hospitals throughout the country owing to the massive brain drain.

28   War veterans ask government for a 300 per cent increase in their monthly pensions; Zanu PF youths camped at the Norton police station continue to burn, beat and intimidate residents of the area; army and police are installed and impose a curfew.

30   Six people are murdered in political violence in September 2001.

OCTOBER 2001

2   Sixteen farm invaders burn down 70 workers' houses in Virginia; 100 workers are camped in the bush; the Supreme Court issues an interim ruling allowing government to proceed with land acquisition.

4   The government rules out the establishment of an independent electoral commission.

5   Libya provides Zimbabwe with US$90 million of fuel. Newspapers report that Libya will be paid with 8 000 ha of land, safari operations, a major hotel group and two financial institutions.

10   Government announces price controls on bread, cooking oil, margarine, soap, chicken, beef, pork, roller meal and generic drugs; timber plantations worth Z$15 million are destroyed in fires started by war veterans and government supporters in the Eastern Highlands; the National Merchant Bank reports that the manufacturing sector has shrunk by 5,4 per cent in the first six months of 2001.

12   War veterans burn down a farmhouse in Chegutu and slash newly planted tobacco seedlings; Morgan Tsvangirai's convoy is attacked and stoned by 50 government supporters en route to Kadoma.

16   Eight schools close in Gokwe as teachers flee after being beaten by war veterans.

17   Hundreds of casual workers in bakeries are laid off as producers slow down production due to price controls.

18   War veterans and government supporters raid shops in Bulawayo and force owners to adhere to price controls even if goods were bought at old prices; three million people face starvation in the Midlands, Masvingo and Matabeleland.

25   Sixty farm invaders storm a Nyabira farm, steal two tractors and assault numerous workers; Commonwealth Foreign Ministers arrive in the country to see if Abuja conditions are being adhered to.

26   Passengers on buses have maize impounded at road blocks by police and war veterans.

29   Commonwealth Heads say they will not release funds for land reform in Zimbabwe as agreed at Abuja until

investigations are made into the breakdown of law and order in Zimbabwe.

30   A US judge rules that Zanu PF are liable for murder and torture – the ruling is made in favour of five Zimbabweans whose relations have been murdered in the past year; three people are murdered in political violence in October 2001.

NOVEMBER 2001

1   Bulawayo war veteran Cain Nkala appears in the Magistrates Court with nine others on charges of the abduction and disappearance of MDC polling agent Patrick Nabanyama in June 2000. Nkala is remanded out of custody.

3   Villagers in Gokwe flee their homes as government supporters assault and torture people they suspect of being opposition supporters.

5   Amnesty International appeals to the EU and Commonwealth to put pressure on President Mugabe to restore law and order in Zimbabwe; Bulawayo war veteran Cain Nkala is abducted from his home, in front of his wife, by ten men. Reports indicate that Nkala had information which could pinpoint the perpetrators of the abduction and presumed murder of MDC polling agent Patrick Nabanyama.

7   Seventy-five armed police descend on the MDC offices in Bulawayo, order employees out and say they are searching for guns and the murderer of Cain Nkala.

8   *Daily News* founders Nyarota and Mbanga are arrested at dawn on shareholding queries into the newspaper.

13   The decomposing body of Cain Nkala is found in a shallow grave 40 km south-west of Bulawayo.

15   ZBC Radio 1 closes down and re-opens as Sport FM; the army offers land on commercial farms to all serving soldiers.

17   Twenty-three farms are listed for compulsory acquisition by the government; 500 war veterans escorted by police go on the rampage in Bulawayo town; they burn down the MDC offices, stone cars and beat up people.

20   Terrorism charges against Morgan Tsvangirai are declared unconstitutional by the Supreme Court.

26   A second-year university student dies after being assaulted by uniformed soldiers and thrown from a moving train outside Harare.

27   Two MDC men tell a Bulawayo High Court judge that they were tortured by police and forced to confess to the murder of Cain Nkala.

29   Police Commissioner Chihuri tells a Shamva farmer to vacate his property as he is now the new owner; the CFU reports that 50 farmers have been given 90-day eviction notices; war veterans descend on old-age homes across Zimbabwe and demand 30 per cent pay increases for workers at these institutions.

30   The Manicaland MDC spokesman is abducted, tortured and dumped in the bush outside Rusape; the ZHR Forum (Zimbabwe Human Rights) releases a report on political violence for the period January to November 2001. Statistics show: Deaths & Executions: 41; Extortion: 31; Intimidation and threats: 262; Kidnapping and disappearances: 307; Property damage and threat: 537; Torture: 2 126; Unlawful detention: 992; five people are murdered in political violence in November 2001.

DECEMBER 2001

1   A 51-year-old Gokwe woman accuses police of not arresting the men who murdered her husband, saying the killers were known government supporters and had remained un-apprehended for over a month.

3   A Chegutu farm is raided by 300 war veterans who seriously assault 20 workers and burn down 42 houses, accusing the people of being opposition supporters. Police were informed but no arrests were made.

4   Nelson Mandela says that President Mbeki's 'quiet diplomacy' policy with Mugabe has not worked and calls for a free and fair election in Zimbabwe; a 76-year-old headman flees his home in Gokwe after being stripped of his traditional position by war veterans who accused him of supporting the MDC.

7   The Catholic Church publicly appeals to the government to denounce violence and respect people's right to free choice;

	the Supreme Court orders Registrar General Tobaiwa Mudede to hold long-overdue mayoral and council elections in Harare before 11 February.
10	The MDC wins mayoral elections in Chegutu.
12	Six detectives and three truckloads of armed riot police raid the home of Morgan Tsvangirai just after midnight. The search warrant bears the wrong address and the search lasts an hour but yields nothing.
13	Zanu PF holds its annual congress at the Victoria Falls, 7 000 delegates attend at a cost of Z$440 million; Vice President Simon Muzenda tells people in Chipinge that if Zanu PF is not re-elected the electricity projects to the area will cease.
14	Listing of 268 farms for compulsory acquisition by government; Morgan Tsvangirai is arrested by armed police at 5.30 am and charged with being in possession of a walkie-talkie radio without a licence; the Public Order and Security Act is gazetted, making it a punishable offence to criticise the President, government, police or army; and to publish or publicly make statements which undermine confidence in the defence or economy of the country. Public gatherings may only be held with police permission; identity documents must be carried at all times.
18	Inflation hits 103 per cent; 500 government youths and members of the Border Gezi Youth Brigade besiege Chegutu Council Offices and refuse to allow the new MDC mayor to be sworn in; farm manager Duncan Cooke is hospitalised after being axed in the head by war veterans and Agritex officials on a farm in Mtepatepa.
20	Newly resettled farmers sell fertiliser given to them by the government in order to raise money to survive; youths from the Border Gezi training centre assault a doctor and physical therapist at the Ruwa Rehabilitation Centre outside Harare shortly after a Christmas party, accusing the men of being opposition supporters; two MDC members are murdered (one beheaded) in Magunje and Karoi by members of the Zanu PF Youth Brigade.
21	US President Bush signs into law the Zimbabwe Democracy Bill which imposes travel bans and freezes the assets of President Mugabe and senior Zanu PF cabinet members.

27   Mobs of youths (some as young as ten) who openly admit
        to having been paid by the government go through
        Masvingo town confiscating and tearing up copies of the
        Daily News.
31   The Ministry of Lands begins publishing names of
        beneficiaries in the land resettlement scheme; ten people
        are murdered in political violence in December 2001.

JANUARY 2002

4   Justice David Bartlett resigns from the bench; a mob of 50
        government supporters attacks homes of MDC supporters
        in the Harare suburbs of Glen Norah and Kuwadzana.
5   Graduates from the Gezi training camps loot grocery shops
        and stalls and destroy 70 houses occupied by MDC
        supporters in Harare; Gezi graduates assault MDC
        supporters in Ruwa and Chinoyi.
7   Security forces (police, army and war veterans) get their
        pay doubled.
9   Zanu PF defeated in Parliament when Electoral
        Amendments Bill is not passed; Gezi graduates mount
        roadblocks, demand Zanu PF cards and seal off the towns
        of Bindura, Chinoyi and Karoi; Parliament passes the
        General Laws Amendment Bill and the Public Order and
        Security Bill.
10   Defence Commander General Zvinavashe says the armed
        forces will only support a political leader who fought in the
        war for independence.
11   Farms around the country are raided by the government.
        Maize stocks intended for workers and livestock are seized.
12   Gapwuz (General Agricultural and Plantation Workers'
        Union) says 10 000 children have been denied an education
        as the fast-track land resettlement scheme closes farm
        schools; 23 farmers evicted from their homes and properties
        in Mashonaland Central in the last week.
15   Karoi farm workers are beaten under their feet with barbed
        wire by government supporters.
16   MDC MP attacked by 20 government supporters and
        stabbed in the stomach.
18   Forty people take refuge in a safe house in Harare after

fleeing political violence in UMP constituency; the Amani
Trust say they are now caring for 1 000 people who have
been displaced by political violence across the country;
immigration officials say 300 people a day are leaving the
country and not returning.

20   At least 30 schools close in south-eastern Zimbabwe after
Zanu PF supporters repeatedly intimidate teachers, invade
classrooms and demand protection fees.

21   Eighteen people are injured by government militants who
prevent an MDC rally from taking place in Bulawayo.

26   High Court orders that voting in the coming elections can
take place anywhere and not just in people's constituencies.
Government says it will contest the ruling.

30   President Mugabe issues a decree overruling the Supreme
Court decision on dates for the Harare mayoral election,
saying the mayoral election will be held concurrently with
presidential elections on 9-10 March.

31   Eighteen people are murdered in political violence in
January 2002.

FEBRUARY 2002

1   Access to Information and Protection of Privacy Bill is
passed in Parliament, which amongst other things bans
foreign journalists from residing in Zimbabwe and
prohibits local journalists from working without a
government licence.

8   Three MDC MPs are abducted, beaten and tortured in
Nkayi after distributing leaflets.

9   The Zimbabwe government bans election observers from
the UK, Germany, Sweden, Denmark, Finland and Holland.

12   Fifty Zanu PF supporters raid MDC offices in Buhera and
steal T-shirts and literature worth half a million dollars. A
police spokesman is recorded as saying: 'We are under strict
instructions from our bosses not to attend to MDC cases.'

13   Morgan Tsvangirai is detained and searched at Harare
airport and accused of travelling on a forged passport.

14   Nine thousand Zanu PF youths camp at community halls
and civic venues around Bulawayo city to campaign for
Mugabe; they mount roadblocks and demand party cards,

petrol bomb and burn houses, stone cars and seize identity documents of people suspected to be supporters of the opposition; leading journalist Basildon Peta flees the country saying he fears for his life.

17   Head of the EU observer team, Pierre Schori, has his visa withdrawn and leaves the country; eleven church parishioners and clergymen, praying for peace, are arrested for holding a gathering without police permission.

18   Zanu PF youths rampage through Gweru after a government rally, smashing windows, looting shops and destroying homes of anyone they suspect of being opposition supporters.

19   EU imposes smart sanctions on Mugabe and 19 other senior Zanu PF officials; all EU election observers are withdrawn from Zimbabwe; Zanu PF youths stone MDC offices in Harare and assault passers-by.

21   Two busloads of Zanu PF supporters attack MDC offices in Chegutu, stone cars and assault passers-by.

23   Two hundred Zanu PF supporters stone the MDC offices in Kwekwe: 30 people are injured; two South African election observers are in the building during the attack. The US imposes a travel ban and freezes the assets of Mugabe and other senior Zanu PF officials; the Media Monitoring Project says that video footage claiming Morgan Tsvangirai is discussing assassinating President Mugabe has been doctored, cut, edited and rearranged.

24   Leader of South African observers, Sam Motsuenyane, refuses to acknowledge that Zanu PF supporters attacked his monitors, instead calling them an 'amorphous mob'; Zanu PF mobs evict farmers from their homes in Chinoyi, Chegutu and Raffingora.

25   SADC observers have vehicles stoned and windscreens smashed near Chinoyi; three observers are injured.

26   The MDC MP for Chipinge north is stoned and assaulted by Zanu PF supporters.

27   Fifty MDC trainee polling agents are attacked at a mission school in Gweru and beaten with stones, logs and machetes; polling stations in urban centres are to be reduced by 30-40 per cent.

28   Fourteen people are murdered in political violence in February 2002.

MARCH 2002

1   Armed police raid MDC offices and arrest 17.

2   Supreme Court Judge Ebrahim resigns from the bench days after declaring electoral amendments illegal.

4   The Commonwealth appoints a troika to consider election observers' reports and take action on behalf of the grouping. The troika consists of Australian Prime Minister Howard, South African President Mbeki and Nigerian President Obasanjo.

5   The army will control all aspects of the elections, including handling and movement of ballot boxes; police raid MDC Mutare offices and seize 210 kg of maize intended to feed displaced opposition supporters.

6   President Mugabe issues an edict reinstating election legislation overthrown by the Supreme Court a week before. One of the clauses allows only government-appointed officials to be election monitors.

7   Retired army general Gula Ndebele, who heads the Electoral Supervisory Committee, cannot answer questions at a press conference from the media and diplomats on how many ballot papers have been printed, where polling stations will be located, who had monitored balloting by army and police voters, or why people were still being registered to vote up to one week before the elections; 600 Zanu PF supporters armed with whips and axes burn down and completely destroy 25 houses in St Peter's village outside Bulawayo, accusing residents of not attending a government rally; only 300 out of 1 200 internal independent election observers are offered accreditation by the government.

9-10   Voting in the presidential election takes place. Queues in urban areas are up to 2 km long and people wait for up to 20 hours without reaching the front. At some urban polling stations as few as five people per hour cast their ballots.

11   Judge rules that voting should be extended to a third day: election officials claim they have not been informed and

baton-wielding riot police chase voters away; some polling stations in Harare reopen, but not until 11 am.

13   Robert Mugabe of Zanu PF is announced the winner of the presidential election; reports and evidence begin coming in of ballot boxes disappearing and then reappearing stuffed with more ballots than had officially been declared; one constituency in Bulawayo records over 11 000 extra ballots having appeared in a supposedly sealed box.

14   Over 1 400 people have been arrested over the election weekend, most of whom are MDC polling agents and volunteers; US President Bush says he does not recognise the election results.

15   Commonwealth observers report the election was neither free nor fair; farmers are evicted from their homes by Zanu PF supporters in Chegutu, Lions Den, Banket, Raffingora, Marondera, Wedza and Bulawayo.

18   Tsvangirai spurns offers by Zanu PF to form a government of national unity while violence continues; Marondera farm guard is murdered by war veterans and farm manager severely assaulted; commercial farmer Terry Ford is murdered after being tied to a tree in his garden, bludgeoned repeatedly and then shot; three MDC supporters in Chipinge are beaten to death; church leaders from the WCC declare the elections were neither free nor fair.

19   Switzerland freezes the assets of Zanu PF officials.

20   The Commonwealth suspends Zimbabwe for a year on recommendations from the appointed troika.

21   Ghana's Foreign Minister supports Zimbabwe's suspension from the Commonwealth.

23   Z$150 million worth of property is damaged or looted by Zanu PF supporters on 15 farms in Wedza in a week.

25   The Zimbabwe Human Rights Forum report on political violence for the period 1 January to 25 March 2002 is released. Statistics are as follows: unlawful detention – 88; deaths and executions – 49; school closures – 48; intimidation and threats – 223; kidnapping – 208; disappearances – 28; rape – 5; property damage – 414; torture – 880; unlawful arrest – 99.

28   The London *Daily Telegraph*'s reporter Peta Thornycroft is
      arrested; Information Minister Jonathan Moyo threatens
      the *Daily News,* saying that nobody should be allowed to
      publish stories suggesting the necessity of a presidential
      poll rerun; MDC polling agent is beaten to death by police
      and soldiers at Ruda police base in Mutare; Australia cancel
      their scheduled cricket tour of Zimbabwe.
30   Anglican Bishop Kunonga's name is added to the US
      sanctions list: riot police fire teargas at Bulawayo residents
      who had attacked a Zanu PF torture base.
31   Agriculture Minister Made announces that government will
      grow winter maize under irrigation, but experts dismiss the
      claim as uneconomic; 20 people are murdered in political
      violence in March 2002.

APRIL 2002
2   RW Johnson, an Oxford University doctoral graduate who
      was in Zimbabwe for the elections, says the sudden
      increase from 2,4 to 2,9 million votes is totally inexplicable.
3   South African-brokered talks between Zanu PF and the
      MDC commence; 1 000 MDC supporters are displaced in
      Zaka and Gutu after Zanu PF militants continue violent
      retribution; Zanu PF supporters engage in retribution in
      Gokwe, where houses are burnt and MDC supporters are
      driven out of the area.
5   After holding a workshop on gender issues 344 women,
      some pregnant and many accompanied by young children,
      are arrested and held for two days; seven Karoi farms have
      property worth Z$17 million looted in a week; the National
      Employment Council reports that 53 184 farm workers have
      been displaced in Mashonaland West owing to farm
      takeovers.
6   Home Affairs Minister John Nkomo warns people not to
      take part in an NCA demonstration pressing for a new
      constitution; soldiers in armoured vehicles move into
      Gweru suburbs and raid nightclubs, and scores are injured;
      MDC MP for Zengeza is attacked in his bedroom by six
      men armed with AK rifles; NCA street demonstrations are
      met with massive army and police resistance – 64 people

are arrested; shop owners in Rusape are given a letter by a Zanu PF official ordering them to reserve any maize delivered for Zanu PF officials, police, war veterans and members of the CIO.

8   Hundreds are forced to flee their homes after 100 Zanu PF militants are bussed into the small mining town of Zvishavane to intimidate MDC supporters.

9   Ghana declares the elections were neither free nor fair; NAACP (National Association for the Advancement of Coloured People) President and CEO sends a letter of protest to the Zimbabwe ambassador to the US. Kwesi Mfume says: ' You cannot run a democracy by jailing the opposition and everyone who disagrees with you.'

10   Zimbabwe bankers say Z$16 billion will be needed for the remainder of 2002 to feed 7,8 million starving people in the country; villagers in Murambinda (Manicaland) are accused of being opposition supporters and are forced to flee their homes after uniformed soldiers terrorise them at night; Registrar General Tobaiwa Mudede announces revised election results – when journalists query discrepancies at the press briefing he refuses to clarify figures and has a *Daily News* reporter escorted out; Catholics denounce the elections saying they were not free and fair; Zanu PF mobs attack MDC polling agents in Mwenezi.

11   War veteran leader Andrew Ndlovu is accused of stealing Z$800 000 for the war vets company ZEXCOM; Registrar General Tobaiwa Mudede's office apologises for disenfranchising white voters.

12   The MDC lodges a 135-page affidavit in the High Court demanding the annulment of election results; armed riot police evict 80 settlers from a Marondera farm in preparation for takeover by Minister Sekeremayi.

14   Chief Justice Godfrey Chidyausiku is added to the US sanctions list, receives a travel ban and has his assets frozen.

15   Marauding Zanu PF supporters close down the Binga council offices, accusing workers of supporting the MDC.

16   Editor in Chief of the *Daily News*, Geoff Nyarota, is arrested and charged under the Access to Information Bill for publishing stories concerning election results; New Zealand

imposes travel bans on Mugabe and senior Zanu PF officials.

18   MDC refused access to electoral roll; editor of the *Independent*, Iden Wetherall, and a journalist are charged with criminal defamation for publishing a story implicating Mugabe's wife's brother in land invasions; US imposes arms embargo on Zimbabwe.

21   Mr and Mrs Bayley finally leave their farm after being barricaded into the house by government militants for 37 days. Mr Bayley is in urgent need of medical attention; President Mugabe's customised Mercedes S600 worth Z$250 million arrives in the country; economists say land resettlement policies are dumping people in the wilderness.

22   Youth brigade members descend on Chinoyi University and 180 students flee; Agriculture Minister Joseph Made warns his officials not to get in the way of the land reform programme.

23   Thirty war veterans burn six houses and 12 tobacco barns belonging to MDC members; farm workers are left homeless; Marondera farmer Guy Cartwright is evicted from his undesignated farm by Marondera East MP Brigadier Mutinhiri, thus becoming the latest of 150 farmers illegally evicted from their farms since the elections; Libyans receive 10 000 hectares of farm land and a block of flats in exchange for Zimbabwe's next consignment of fuel; 23 NCA demonstrators are arrested by riot police while staging a protest demanding a new constitution.

25   War Veterans' Association secretary for projects, Andrew Ndlovu, threatens Asian businessmen, calling them economic looters and telling them to hand over their property or risk having it seized.

26   President Mugabe gives amnesty to 4 998 prisoners; Zanu PF sued for Z$2,4 billion in the US for perpetrating violence against five Zimbabweans murdered in 2000; violence increases ahead of Kadoma mayoral poll.

30   Evictions by war veterans leave 1 300 farm workers and their families out in the open; four people are murdered in political violence in April 2002.

MAY 2002

2   Two *Daily News* journalists are arrested under the Media Bill.

3   War veteran Andrew Ndlovu issues eviction letters to farmers; 250 farmers have been forcibly evicted from their homes and farms since elections.

5   Headlands farmer, Cheryl Jones, is shot and critically injured at her farm gate.

7   *Daily News* columnist arrested.

10   Teachers Union reporting on its members says in the last year: 20 000 kidnapped and tortured by government supporters; 14 000 displaced and accused of supporting the MDC; 190 female teachers raped; 107 503 teachers paid extortion money to government supporters; Parliament reconvened for a day to ratify amendments to the Land Acquisition Act, then adjourned until August; Zanu PF pulls out of talks brokered by South Africa and Nigeria; West Nicholson Wheeler family evicted from their farm after being barricaded in for 24 days, losing farm assets and 700 tonnes of farm produce worth over Z$22 million.

12   *Independent* journalist detained.

14   Israeli riot control equipment arrives in Harare, including tankers, water cannons, gas masks and microscopic 'laser guns'.

15   Police pick up 270 farm workers and their families camped in Harare and being supported by charitable organisations and dump them on a Marondera farm; after clash with war veterans many of the workers flee into the bush.

17   Three *Standard* journalists are arrested.

18   List of 181 Zanu PF officials who seized or were given the pick of Zimbabwe's farms.

22   Editor in Chief of the *Daily News*, Geoff Nyarota, is arrested again.

24   Government announces it has started evicting settlers from unlisted and de-listed farms, but there is no evidence of this happening on the ground; only four weeks' supply of wheat is left in the country.

27   Eighty-nine-year-old farmer Thomas Bayley dies in his sleep one week after surviving a 30-day siege barricaded into his farmhouse.

28   Agriculture Minister Made threatens to de-register the
        Commercial Farmers Union.

JUNE 2002

2   Commercial farmer Charles Anderson is fatally shot in his
        Glendale farmhouse.

ZIMBABWE'S ROLL OF HONOUR

We remember them. We mourn them. We salute them.

All the men and women listed here have been killed in political violence in Zimbabwe since March 2000. In almost all cases their deaths have been brutal and exceedingly violent, following protracted and barbaric torture. Some were axed to death, others had their heads cut off with garden spades or were beaten and kicked until they died. Victims were hugely outnumbered, unable to protect themselves and had no one to turn to for help. They have not died in vain – the struggle for democracy continues. Grateful thanks to Primrose Matambanadzo at the Zimbabwe Human Rights Forum for assistance in checking and updating the list.

2000

1	26 March	Edwin Gomo. (MDC) Bindura.
2	26 March	Robert Musoni. Mazowe West.
3	2 April	Doreen Marufu. (MDC) Mazowe.
4	4 April	Tinashe Chakwenya. ZR Police constable. Marondera.
5	14 April	Tichaona Chiminya. (MDC) Buhera North.
6	15 April	David Stevens. (MDC) Commercial farmer. Murehwa.
7	15 April	Talent Mabika. (MDC) Buhera North.
8	18 April	Martin Olds. Commercial farmer. Bubi-Umguza.
9	20 April	Julius Andoche. Farm foreman. Murehwa South.

10	23 April	Peter Kareza. (MDC) Shamva.
11	24 April	Mr Banda. (MDC) Shamva.
12	25 April	Nicholas Chaitama. (MDC) Kariba.
13	25 April	Luckson Kanyurira. (MDC) Kariba.
14	30 April	Matthew Pfebve. (MDC) Mount Darwin.
15	6 May	Tapera. Macheke.
16	7 May	Laben Chiwara. Harare.
17	7 May	Allan Dunn. Commercial farmer. Seke.
18	13 May	Alex Chisasa. ZR Police. Chipinge South.
19	14 May	John Weeks. Commercial farmer. Seke.
20	16 May	Takundwa Chipunza. (MDC) Budiriro, Harare.
21	17 May	Joseph Mandeya. (MDC) Mutasa.
22	17 May	Mationa Mushaya. (United Party) Mutoko.
23	17 May	Onias Mushaya. (United Party) Mutoko.
24	27 May	Kufandaedza Musekiwa. Marondera West.
25	29 May	Thadeus Rukini. (MDC) Masvingo.
26	31 May	Tony Oates. Commercial farmer. Zvimba North.
27	10 June	Leo Jeke. Masvingo.
28	10 June	Fainos Zhou. (MDC) Mberengwa.
29	11 June	Mr Chinyere. (MDC)
30	19 June	Constantine Mafemeruke. Kariba.
31	19 June	Patrick Nabanyama. (MDC) Bulawayo. Abducted, presumed dead.
32	20 June	Zeke Chigagura. (MDC) Gokwe East.
33	20 June	Tichaona Tadyanemhandu. (MDC) Hurungwe.
34	23 June	Wonder Manhango. (MDC) Gokwe North.
35	27 June	Matyatya. (MDC) Gweru.
36	29 June	Mandishona Mutyanda. (MDC) Kwekwe.
37	June	Nhamo Gwase. (MDC) Murehwa South.
38	23 July	Willem Botha. Commercial farmer. Seke.
39	27 July	Itayi Maguwu. (MDC) Harare.
40	9 August	Samson Mbewe. Farm worker. Goromonzi.
41	14 September	Obert Guvi. Hurungwe West.
42	19 November	Lemani Chapurunga. Marondera West.
43	19 November	Rimon Size. Marondera West.
44	12 December	Henry Elsworth. Commercial farmer. Kwekwe.
45	13 December	Howard Kareza. (MDC) Shamva.
46	31 December	Bernard Gara. (Zanu PF) Bikita West, Masvingo.

2001

47	16 January	Ropafadzo Manyame. (MDC) Bikita.
48	22 February	Fr Peter Wayner. Masvingo.
49	4 March	Gloria Olds. Commercial farmer. Bubi-Umguza.
50	23 March	Eswat Chihumbiri. Muzarabani.
51	30 March	Ndonga Mupesa. (MDC) Muzarabani.
52	March	Robson Chirima. (MDC) Muzarabani.
53	March	Peter Mataruse. (MDC) Muzarabani.
54	1 May	Richard Chikwenya. (MDC) Buhera North.
55	4 May	Misheck Mwanza. (MDC) Zvimba North.
56	18 May	Winnie Nyambare. Guruve.
57	9 June	Zondani Dumukani. Farm worker. Harare.
58	2 July	John Chakwenya. Epworth, Harare.
59	3 July	James Nyika. (MDC) Hatfield, Harare.
60	3 July	John Manomera. (MDC) Hatfield, Harare.
61	22 July	Peter Mandindishi. Bindura.
62	27 July	Gilson Gwenzi. (MDC) Mwenezi.
63	2 August	Thomas Katema. Harare.
64	6 August	Robert Cobbet. Commercial farmer. Kwekwe.
65	9 September	Vusumuzi Mukweli. (MDC) Gokwe South.
66	15 September	Alexio Nyamadzawo. Wedza.
67	16 September	Fanuel Madzvimbo. Wedza.
68	18 September	Osbon Ziweni. (MDC) Masvingo.
69	27 September	Nyathi Mbuso. (ZNLWA) Nkayi.
70	September	Felix Zava. (MDC) Headmaster. Chikomba.
71	15 October	Hilary Matema. Guruve South.
72	29 October	Limukani Lupahla. (Zanu PF) Lupane.
73	30 October	Mhondiwa Chitemerere. (MDC) Murehwa South.
74	5 November	Cain Nkala. (ZNLWA) Bulawayo.
75	10 November	Ravengai Sikhucha. (MDC) Mberengwa East.
76	11 November	Johannes Sikele. Resettled farmer. Masvingo.
77	19 November	Kufa Rukara. (MDC) Silobela, Gokwe North.
78	24 November	Lameck Chemvura. UZ student. Manicaland.
79	6 December	Michael Mugodoki. Farm guard. Chikomba.
80	9 December	Augustus Chacha. (MDC) Gokwe.
81	20 December	Titus Nheya. (MDC) Karoi.
82	20 December	Milton Chambati. (MDC) Magunge.

83	23 December	Trymore Midzi. (MDC) Bindura.
84	24 December	Rambisai Nyika. (MDC) Gokwe South.
85	25 December	Willis Dhliwayo. (ZNLWVA) Chipinge North.
86	29 December	Moffat Soka Chiwaura. (MDC) Bindura.
87	31 December	Shepherd Tigere. (MDC) Gokwe South.
88	December	Laban Chiweta. (MDC) Bindura.

2002

89	9 January	Mr Chitehwe. (ZNLWA) Hatfield, Harare.
90	9 January	Amos Mapingure. Bikita East.
91	9 January	Gibson Masarira. (Zanu PF) Zaka East
92	13 January	Kenneth Matope. (MDC) Guruve.
93	15 January	Simwanja Mijoni. Kwekwe.
94	17 January	Isaac Munikwa. (Zanu PF) Zaka East.
95	18 January	Kuziva Sanyamahwe. (MDC) Murehwa South.
96	19 January	Muchenje Mpofu. (MDC) Mberengwa East.
97	20 January	Richard Chatunga. (MDC) Bikita East.
98	20 January	Richard Maphosa. (Zanu PF) Bikita East.
99	23 January	Unnamed farm guard. Mwenezi.
100	23 January	Unnamed farm guard. Mwenezi.
101	23 January	Solomon Nemaire. (MDC) Makoni.
102	26 January	Mthokozisi Ncube. (MDC) Bulawayo.
103	27 January	Fungisai Mutemaringa. (MDC) Murehwa.
104	30 January	Halaza Sibindi. (MDC) Tsholotsho.
105	30 January	Jameson Sicwe. (MDC) Lupane.
106	January	Joseph Sibindi. (MDC) Bulawayo.
107	February	James Sibanda. (MDC) Nkayi.
108	February	Newman Bhebe. (MDC) Nkayi.
109	2 February	Stephen Maphosa. (Zanu PF) Budiriro, Harare.
110	4 February	Tichaona Katsamudanga. (MDC) Harare North.
111	5 February	Shepherd Ngundu. (MDC) Mount Darwin.
112	6 February	Khape Khumalo. (MDC) Mhondoro.
113	7 February	Henry Moyo. (MDC) Masvingo.
114	8 February	Tariro Nyanzira. (Zanu PF) Buhera North.
115	14 February	Munyaradzi (surname unknown). Marondera East.
116	14 February	Tubadamo Mukakarei. (MDC) Masvingo.
117	16 February	Takatukwa Mupawaenda. Zvimba South.

118 20 February Takesure Nhitsa. (MDC) Rushinga.
119 26 February Unnamed Makokoba. Bulawayo.
120 27 February Lloyd Shelton. (Zanu PF) Chikomba.
121 March   Lawrence Kuvheya. (MDC) Chikomba.
122 March   Edwin Romio. (MDC) Polling agent. Mutoko.
123 1 March   Nqobizita Dube. (MDC) Nkulumane,
                  Bulawayo.
124 2 March   Charles Sibanda. (MDC) Zhombe.
125 3 March   Peter Jeftha. Harare South.
126 8 March   Amos Maseva. (ZNLWVA) Gutu North.
127 12 March   Tafirenyika Gwaze. (MDC) Polling agent.
                  Mutoko.
128 13 March   Funny Mahuni. Kwekwe.
129 15 March   Darlington Vikaveka. (MDC) Marondera East.
130 16 March   Unnamed. (MDC) Chipinge.
131 16 March   Unnamed. (MDC) Chipinge.
132 16 March   Unnamed. (MDC) Chipinge.
133 17 March   Sambani Ncube. (MDC) Hwange.
134 17 March   Owen Manyara. (MDC) Mount Darwin.
135 18 March   Terry Ford. Commercial farmer. Mhondoro.
136 19 March   Ernest Gatsi. (MDC) Guruve.
137 25 March   Donald Jeranyama. (MDC) Polling agent.
                  Mutasa.
138 26 March   Simon Pilosi. (MDC) Zvimba.
139 29 March   Fanuel White. (MDC) Polling agent. Guruve.
140 2 April   Micah Chidari. (Zanu PF) Mhondoro.
141 4 April   Noah Gwidzima. (Zanu PF) Makoni North.
142 4 April   Petros Jeka. (MDC) Polling agent. Masvingo.
143 27 April   Davis Mtetwa. (MDC) Zengeza.
144 2 May   Tipason Madhoba. (MDC) Polling agent.
                  Gokwe.
145 5 May   Genus Ngamira. (MDC) Bindura.

BIBLIOGRAPHY

BOOKS

Bernstein, Hilda (1989). *The World That Was Ours. The Story of the Rivonia Trials*. SA Writers. London.

Fredrikse, Julie (1982). *None But Ourselves. Masses vs Media in the Making Of Zimbabwe*. ZPH. Harare.

Garlake, Peter (1987). *The Painted Caves. An Introduction to the Prehistoric Art of Zimbabwe*. Modus. Harare.

Gelfand, M. *et al.* (1985). *The Traditional Medical Practitioner in Zimbabwe. His Principles of Practice & Pharmacopoeia*. Mambo Press. Zimbabwe.

Godwin, Peter & Hancock, Ian (1993). *Rhodesians Never Die*. Baobab Books, Harare.

IDAF (1977). *Zimbabwe, The Facts About Rhodesia*. International Defence & Aid Fund for Southern Africa.

Keneally, Thomas (1982). *Schindler's Ark*. Hodder & Stoughton. London

Lan, David (1985). *Guns and Rain. Guerillas and Spirit Mediums in Zimbabwe*. ZPH. Harare.

Martin, David & Johnson, Phyllis (1981). *The Struggle for Zimbabwe: The Chimurenga War*. Ravan Press. Johannesburg.

Mitchell, Diana (1980). *Who's Who. African Nationalist Leaders in Zimbabwe*. Books of Rhodesia. Harare.

Ranger, Terence (1985). *Peasant Consciousness and Guerilla War in Zimbabwe*. ZPH. Harare.

Russell, Alec (2000). *Big Men Little People. Encounters in Africa*. Macmillan. London.

Sparks, Allister (1995). *Tomorrow is Another Country*. Heinemann.

UNESCO (1975). *Racism and Apartheid in Southern Africa – Rhodesia*. Unesco Press, Paris.

NEWSPAPERS, PERIODICALS AND OTHER PRINTED PUBLICATIONS.

Commercial Farmers Union: Farm Invasions and Security Reports, Zimbabwe.

Daily News Online, Zimbabwe.

Daily News, Zimbabwe.

Daily Telegraph Online, UK.

De Week, Holland.

Financial Gazette, Zimbabwe.

Guardian Online, UK.

Herald, Zimbabwe.

Le Figaro, France.

Standard, Zimbabwe.

Sunday Times Online, UK.

The Farmer Magazine, Zimbabwe.

The Times Online, UK.

Washington Post Online, UK.

Zimbabwe Human Rights Forum Reports on Political Violence, Zimbabwe.

ZW News, daily Online News reports.

ACKNOWLEDGEMENTS

My thanks go to Zimbabwe's farmers and their employees who have seen hell and lived with it for 27 months – and continue to do so. The farmers named below have been brave enough to let me tell their stories. In doing so they have relived the horrors and revisited their nightmares. Their tolerance, endurance and courage have been inspirational. This is their story and my profound thanks go to: Alan and Anthea Bradley, Micky and Myrtle Buswell, Locci and Tina de Jongh, Stuart and Lise Gemmill, Ox Hacking, Ian and Marjo Hardy, Tonia and Brendan Jowett, Kerry Kay, Steve Krynauw, Gary and Jenny Luke, Johan and Mary Jane Muller, Laura Olds, John Osborne, Mandy Retzlaff, Jon Jon Rutherford, Hilda and Lothar Sittig, Maria Stevens.

This book would not have been written without the love, friendship, support, encouragement and assistance of: Pauline Henson, who was there for me every single day, cutting, researching, translating, editing and recording; Chris Garner, my Cape Town Cavalier who has given his heart and soul to saving Zimbabwe, built the *African Tears* web site and continues to allow me to invade his life and share his innermost thoughts; Linda Grey, who would not let me give up, who showed me the daily anguish of standing by your beliefs and principles – you will not regret it; Steve Krynauw, friend and soul mate.

There are hundreds of people who have supported me and helped me survive two years of Zimbabwe's horrors, so many that I cannot possibly list them all. Every e-mail, letter, card and call has been appreciated, every offer of help is treasured. My respect and thanks go to Bill Saidi of the *Daily News* for agreeing to write the Foreword and also to the dozens of journalists, reporters, editors, human rights organisations, displaced and ex-Zimbabweans and people who care all over the world for helping to expose this crisis. My special thanks to those who have put me on their web sites, lobbied their MPs, and sent unceasing e-mails, food parcels and gifts. Please do not be offended if you are not named – I have not forgotten your help or friendship. My special thanks to Su Balcombe, Ann Benham, Elizabeth Bishop, Gorry Bowes Taylor, Mike Clark, Karen Collins, Fiona Duthie, Gill Dilmitis, Neil Douglas, Louise and Mike Dykins, Henry Faber, Colleen Henderson, Bill and Ann Glover, Ann Harben, Jax Hayward, Ann Hein, Mike Jones, Ray Jones, David Kilgour MP, Fr Arthur Lewis, Arnold Parkinson, Ronnie Machlachlan, Primrose Matambanadzo, Nola Nothling, Stefania Oliviero, Jeff Rense, Vikki Rolfe, John Russell, Simon Spooner, Rod Stevens, Lucy and Heather Tarr, Di Thornton, Linda Townsend, Elaine van der Merwe, Bert van Rhijn, Len Wass.

Above all, my thanks go to all the ordinary Zimbabweans who are determined not to give up their fight for democracy.

INDEX